NORTH STAR
STATEHOUSE

View through the stair halls from the Senate chamber to the Supreme Court chamber.

NORTH STAR STATEHOUSE

AN ARMCHAIR GUIDE
TO THE
MINNESOTA STATE CAPITOL

THOMAS O'SULLIVAN

POGO PRESS

ISBN 1-880654-07-5.

Library of Congress Catalogue Card No. 94-66863.

Color photographs by Bob Firth.

Cover design by Earl Gutnik.

Black and white photography credits: Mike Hazard, pages 18 and 98; National Academy of Design, page 6; and all others, courtesy of the Minnesota Historical Society.

Back cover photograph: House of Representatives chamber before restoration in 1989-90.

Front cover chair logo: armchair from the Minnesota State Capitol.

Recognition

$\mathscr{T}$HE AUTHOR and publisher will donate a portion of the proceeds from sales of this book to the Minnesota Historical Society, in recognition of its work in preserving the Minnesota State Capitol, and in interpreting its art, architecture, and history through the tours and programs of its Capitol Historic Site.

For Thea,
a capital kid

Contents

Acknowledgements

$\mathscr{T}$HIS BOOK is the product of a dozen years' fascination with a building. In that time many people have helped me to understand the Minnesota State Capitol's life and art. Patrick Coleman has been a ready source of insights and encouragement, given freely and spiced with sharp humor. Carolyn Kompelien, Brian Pease, and the staff of the Capitol Historic Site have all educated and informed me about the statehouse; their knowledge, enthusiasm, and grace under public pressure are inspiring.

I owe thanks for support and assistance to other colleagues and friends at the Minnesota Historical Society: Carolyn Anderson, James Fogerty, Sherri Gebert Fuller, Anne McDonald, Bonnie Wilson, and the staff of the Research Center. Gary Grefenberg, Mary Duroche, and Paul Mandell of the Capitol Area Architectural and Planning Board shared ideas and information generously. Photographer Mike Hazard made his excellent pictures available to me. Governor Elmer L. Andersen's foreword is an honor of which *North Star Statehouse* is, I hope, worthy.

Four people deserve special thanks, for they did much to make this project possible, enjoyable, and far better than it could have been without their talents. Earl Gutnik offered his fine designer's touch and calm encouragement throughout the endeavor. Bob Firth's magnificent color photographs opened my eyes and mind to the Capitol as a work of art with infinite facets. Finally, Molly and John Harris of Pogo Press gave me firm support, thoughtful editing, genial challenges, and the opportunity to put my ideas to work in this book.

Thomas O'Sullivan
St. Paul, Minnesota
August 26, 1994

Elmer L. Andersen, Governor of Minnesota, 1961-63.

Foreword

*M*INNESOTA HISTORY provides many incidents and characters of which residents or observers can be proud. When it was necessary to participate in battle, Minnesota units did exceptionally well, with Gettysburg one outstanding example. In processes of government, a "squeaky clean" reputation has been well deserved. It was incredible that a state so modest in population and resources of wealth could produce a great national university in the University of Minnesota. The agriculture of our state has also been a leader in productivity and Minnesota industrial research has contributed many innovations nation-wide and world-wide.

Of all these opportunities for pride in our state's accomplishments, the one that looms highest on my list is the building of our state Capitol.

It was such a remarkable concept and achievement that it well deserves full treatment and recording. I am glad that Thomas O'Sullivan has undertaken to do this, and I think it is appropriate that a curator of art at the Minnesota Historical Society has been inspired to do so. Art is closely related to architecture. It is remarkable that the artistic and architectural significance of our state Capitol has endured for nine decades and can still remain such a wonderful example of noble concept and skillful achievement.

The Minnesota State Capitol is a constant inspiration to me. Built only fifty years after our statehood, it represents the tremendous vision and accomplishment of the people of our state. It challenges us to meet the needs of the present day, as they did in theirs, with a similar vision and commitment to future generations. To recapture the vision, to record the accomplishments, and to preserve them for future generations is a marvelous contribution by Thomas O'Sullivan. We are grateful to him for this book.

Elmer L. Andersen
former Governor of Minnesota

Renaissance Statehouse
on the Mississippi

～❦～

$\mathscr{T}$AKE FIFTY STEPS up a granite staircase, pull open a tall, heavy door, and step into the cool vestibule of the Minnesota State Capitol. There on the wall is a plaque that pictures in polished bronze the façade and floor plans of the building, with a table of facts and figures:

CASS GILBERT—ARCHITECT.

TOTAL APPROPRIATION FOR BUILDING AND SITE	$4,500,000.00
GREATEST LENGTH OF BUILDING	434 FEET
GREATEST WIDTH OF BUILDING	229 FEET
HEIGHT FROM GROUND TO TOP OF DOME	223 FEET
EXTERIOR DIAMETER OF DOME	89 FEET
INTERIOR DIAMETER OF DOME	60 FEET

This tally of proud statistics hangs like a museum label on a work of art. And rightfully so. Ever since its completion in 1905, the Capitol has been praised as a masterpiece of American art and architecture at the dawn of the twentieth century.

This book offers its readers—both those who have visited the Capitol, and those who may know it only from a distance—a tour in words and pictures of Minnesota's statehouse. Like a guided tour, this book blends the Capitol's past and present in a mix of history, description, and interpretation. Its illustrations will have to serve some readers as a substitute for seeing the real thing. But those who have climbed the steps to the Capitol in person can best use this book as a field guide to the history and art of a Minnesota landmark.

The Minnesota State Capitol stands at the intersection of high ideals and everyday life. It is home to lofty discourse and petty arguments, graceful allegorical paintings and tons of mundane paperwork. The building has served as Minnesota's statehouse since 1905. That old-fashioned term suggests the dual requirements of a building that is central to the commonwealth. A statehouse has functional *and* symbolic duties. It needs sufficient size and working space to accom-

Vestibule, circa *1913.*

modate the executive, legislative, and judiciary branches of state government. But a statehouse is more than square footage. It is the heart of civic life, and deserves a grandeur of expression that Minnesota's Capitol delivers in design, decoration, and craftsmanship. Its noble spaces and fine materials are reminders to anyone who enters—whether senator or schoolchild—that this is a special place for important business.

Visitors can sense this mix of timeless principles and daily work on a tour of the Capitol. They see it in paintings of classical nudes and state officials. They feel it in the wide stone treads of a grand staircase, or the well-rubbed bronze boot of a Civil War colonel's statue. They hear it in oratory from state chambers and in telephone chatter from offices. Citizens regard the Capitol with greater ambivalence than they feel toward any other building in the state. They sometimes see it only as the place of origin of taxes and meddlesome statutes. But year after year, Minnesotans return to the "showplace of the state," as a Minneapolis newspaper called the Capitol ninety years ago. This is the building Minnesotans show off to their guests, whether foreign dignitaries or cousins up from Iowa. Their love-hate relationship with a building as the symbol and center of government has always been part of the Capitol's story of design, construction, use, and restoration.

The story began in 1893. Minnesotans decided to build a new capitol, their third since Minnesota became a territory in 1849, and a state in 1858. The first Capitol in St. Paul was a two-story brick building, completed in 1853 at Tenth and Cedar Streets. Its low dome and plain Doric columns lent a modest civic touch. The building was twice remodeled to become a more spacious and stylish statehouse in the 1870s, but a fire in 1881 destroyed it totally. The second Capitol was completed on the same site in 1883, to the eclectic design of Minneapolis architect Leroy Buffington. A four-story brick building with stone trim and a tall tower, the second Capitol featured elaborate woodwork in its large chambers. Yet complaints of overcrowding and poor ventilation dogged the building from the start, and a legislative committee recommended construction of a new capitol in 1893. "Buffington's lemon," as architecture critic Larry Millett summed up the second Capitol in echo of its occupants' distaste, housed minor offices and storage spaces until it was razed in 1937/1938. Its political power and architectural glory had long since passed to the stately marble Capitol four blocks north; its site now holds St. Paul's Arts and Science Center.

Selecting a proper site was among the first critical decisions in creating the new Capitol. The Board of State Capitol Commissioners, a seven-member citizen group appointed to oversee the new statehouse, chose land that some thought remote from the heart of St. Paul. While the site of the first and second Capitols seemed undistin-

guished yet businesslike, the new site demanded a brisk walk up
Wabasha Hill. Today the automobile has further exaggerated the site's
isolation. The ten-lane trench of Interstate Highway 94 poses a strong
psychological boundary between the Capitol and downtown streets,
and often a fiercely windy barrier as well. But the commissioners'
choice of the hilltop site still shows genius in the way it lifts the Capitol above its surroundings. It is equally prominent whether one views
it at leisure from a downtown sidewalk or catches glimpses through
the windshield at fifty miles per hour.

The form of the Capitol prompts instant recognition of this building as the center of government. With its imposing size, its symmetrical façade of white marble, and its dome, Minnesota's statehouse follows an architectural model that is virtually imprinted on Americans.
Thirty-two of the nation's state capitols are domed buildings, two
dozen of them in classical revival styles akin to Minnesota's statehouse. A commissioner noted at the laying of the Minnesota cornerstone in 1898 that "public sentiment educated by familiarity with the
great Capitol building at Washington, required that this should be a
domed building, with impressive approaches and an extensive rotunda." All the finalists in the national competition for Minnesota's
capitol proposed some version of the domed statehouse, in styles that
harkened back to European architectural traditions. The winning design by St. Paul architect Cass Gilbert linked Minnesota to the artistic
traditions of the national Capitol in Washington, D. C., the great
buildings of the Renaissance in Italy, and the architectural relics of
classical civilization. This eminent pedigree was intended to stir
pride in the state and to brighten Minnesota's national image, too.
The huge amounts of timber Minnesotans cut or flour they milled did
not alone suffice to show progress, much less culture. "Such a state
and such a people deserve a capitol that they may be proud to exhibit
to a stranger," said a Duluth politician. A monumental and beautiful
capitol building, rivaling the civic landmarks of eastern cities, could
redress the notion of Minnesota as a raw frontier state. This new
Capitol was meant to announce boldly to the world that the state had
arrived, and that aim seemed fulfilled when articles about it appeared
in national magazines soon after its completion.

The man chosen to design the Capitol was uniquely qualified to
make pronouncements in stone on the state's behalf. Cass Gilbert
was born in 1859 in Ohio, but raised in St. Paul. After studying briefly

Cass Gilbert's competition drawing for the Capitol, 1895.

at the Massachusetts Institute of Technology, he refined his eye and his taste by travels through Europe. Gilbert began his professional career as a draftsman in the New York offices of the prestigious firm of McKim, Mead and White. In 1884 he opened an office in St. Paul in a partnership with James Knox Taylor, then worked alone when Taylor was appointed architect to the federal Treasury Department. One can still examine Gilbert's early commissions in St. Paul within a few miles of the Capitol. He designed churches and substantial homes on and near Summit Avenue. Other buildings like the Endicott Building and St. Paul Seminary, as well as churches and railroad stations across Minnesota, attest to Gilbert's early success in the Midwest. They illustrate his mastery of Queen Anne, Romanesque, Colonial Revival and other styles popular in the late nineteenth century. Architectural scholar Sharon Irish summed up Gilbert's approach: "Never a theorist, he instead saw his role as developing solutions to architectural problems, as a provider of services to a client and a public."

These early projects marked Cass Gilbert as talented, versatile, and ambitious—facets of a headstrong personality that would help make the Capitol not just a major building, but a springboard to Gilbert's national career. A contemporary described him as

CASS GILBERT·A·N·A·
BY KENYON COX, 1907·

Portrait of Gilbert by Kenyon Cox, 1907.

a man of distinctive and rather distinguished appearance, somewhat
above middle height, of good figure slightly inclining to corpulence in
his later years, purposely impressive in manner and rather pompous
at times. He spoke well and fluently but without humor, and never
talked above the heads of his clients. It was said in the Century Club
in New York that he could give the most convincing exposition of the
obvious that had ever been heard there.

The testimony of fellow clubmen is apt, for Gilbert moved smoothly among America's men of affairs, and used his connections to good effect throughout his career.

The Capitol project gave Gilbert an extended opportunity to hone his tactical skills, as well as his design sense. With the whole of Minnesota as his client, Gilbert labored under the watchful eyes of the Board of State Capitol Commissioners, the legislature, the newspapers, and the architects of his state. Historian Neil B. Thompson recounts in detail the controversies that attended the creation of the Capitol in his 1974 book, *The Minnesota State Capitol: The Art and Politics of a Public Building*. The resolution of two early controversies illustrates how architecture can be an art of politics and intrigue, as well as an art of spaces and materials, and how Gilbert mastered all its aspects.

The first controversy centered on the selection and role of the Capitol architect. The Board of State Capitol Commissioners was composed of laymen; its vice-president and leader, Channing Seabury, was a civic-minded wholesale grocer. Minnesota's architectural community offered its advice to the gentlemen of the Board at an early date. In 1894 the American Institute of Architects' Minnesota chapter—Cass Gilbert, president—urged the Board not to limit the cost of the Capitol to two million dollars, as its enabling legislation had prescribed. The group further advised that the architect's fee be doubled from two and a half percent to as much as five percent of the building's costs, and that the architect himself supervise the construction. These two suggestions were ultimately adopted by the Board and approved by the legislature.

The Minnesota architects also expressed dissatisfaction with the Board's plan for an open design competition, preferring instead that qualified architects be invited to compete. They did not prevail on this issue, but events of the following months proved them right. An open competition announced in 1894 drew just fifty-six entries, from which the Board's advisers chose five designs with lukewarm praise. With the support of the architectural profession the Board rejected all five designs in 1895, and announced a new competition. This one attracted just forty-one entries, but consulting architect Edmund M. Wheelwright of Boston felt that "The average merit of these designs was much higher than the previous competition." The five designs recommended by Wheelwright included the work of three Minnesota

*Sculptor carving a marble eagle for the Capitol dome
in a shed on the grounds.*

firms—Gilbert, Clarence H. Johnston of St. Paul, and Bassford, Traphagen and Fitzpatrick of St. Paul and Duluth—as well as George R. Mann of St. Louis and Denver's Wendell and Humphreys. Following Seabury's lead, the Board of State Capitol Commissioners then chose Gilbert's design for their statehouse.

The second issue had a more tangible object: selection of the stone for the exterior of the Capitol. Historian Thompson summarized the debate well as a volatile mix of aesthetics, economics and politics. Gilbert had built a skillful case for using the finest marble, the stone of choice for important civic buildings. Aside from its tradition and durability, marble had the brilliant white color the architect demanded, to avoid crowning Wabasha Hill with a gloomy, fortress-like pile (like the granite cathedral that was built nearby soon after the Capitol was completed). The stone Gilbert desired, however, was marble quarried in the state of Georgia. Brilliant white, the stone featured rich veins of black and silver-gray. This was not just an expensive, out-of-state material, but stone from a state many Minnesotans knew best as the scene of Civil War actions in their younger days. Many felt that the use of Georgia marble would add aesthetic insult to economic injury. The choice of a "foreign" material would deprive Minnesota's stone industry of the prestige of the state's foremost building, and take lucrative contracts out of the hands of the quarry owners and stoneworkers of St. Cloud, Little Falls, Mankato, and other cities.

Anticipating strong objections, Gilbert suggested a compromise: Minnesota granite and sandstone for the steps, terraces, and ground floor walls, and Georgia marble for the walls above. The commissioners voted for that combination after days of debate. The use of Georgia stone fueled newspaper attacks nonetheless. The two-stone compromise proved to be less expensive than using only a satisfactory Minnesota granite, and the Georgia stone was shipped in raw blocks so that Minnesota stonecutters could work it. But the public outcry proved to be a trial-by-fire for a building where partisan battles and intra-state rivalries have always been the order of the day.

The visitor who approaches the Capitol today, whether it is gleaming under summer sun or icy white against a deep blue winter sky, will applaud Gilbert's taste in stone and his Board's tenacity in fighting for it. His building is best approached on foot, for the walk affords an opportunity to study the block-long façade. Gilbert's design draws the eye to the center of the building, and *up:* from a wide flight of granite steps, to a loggia of three vast arches, to a blaze of golden sculpture known as the Quadriga. Crowning the whole is a dome of white marble, which brings the building to a height of well over two hundred feet at its gilded pinnacle.

It is this dome that most confidently proclaims the Capitol's presence—not just in Minnesota's capital city, but in architectural tradition as well. In St. Paul, the dome is a local landmark that catches one's eye from far and near. It is visible from the blufftop neighborhoods across the Mississippi valley, and from streets all around the Capitol district. The dome is Gilbert's homage to the Italian Renaissance. He modeled his dome on no less an authority than Michelangelo's dome for the cathedral of St. Peter in Rome. Like that mid-sixteenth century edifice, Gilbert's dome sits atop a drum which features pairs of columns between each window. Like St. Peter's, the Minnesota dome has stone ribs and deeply-carved window moldings on its marble skin, and rises to a columned stone lantern. There are differences, too. Gilbert's dome, far smaller than its inspiration in Rome, has a dozen distinctly American eagles perched on the paired columns around the drum. And the cross that tops St. Peter's has been omitted, in favor of a simple and secular gold sphere.

The dome on the Minnesota statehouse is a worthy emblem for the turn-of-the-century mindset that is known variously as the City Beautiful, Beaux Arts or American Renaissance movement. It is an attitude that aimed to join classical design, based on the architecture of Greece and Rome, to the needs of a coal-fired, steam-driven, city-raising American society. Art theorists like mural painter Kenyon Cox explained that the philosophy he and Gilbert shared "wishes to add link by link to the chain of tradition, but it does not wish to break the chain." "The Classic Spirit is the disinterested search for perfection," he mused. "It is the love of clearness and reasonableness and self-control; it is, above all, the love of permanence and continuity." Writing his impressions of the Minnesota Capitol in *The Architectural Record* in August 1905, Cox called attention to the interplay of different art forms as he compared Gilbert's dome to a time-honored standard of beauty: "This great dome is a vast piece of sculpture upon which the light falls as caressingly as upon the white breast of the Venus de Milo."

Gilbert and his peers were no mere antiquarians, however. Their

Snapshot of Gilbert on the roof during dome construction in 1901.

skin-deep classicism often depended on modern technologies to real-
ize age-old forms. The Capitol dome concealed an innovative structure of steel and brick beneath its marble skin. Gilbert took pride in
this solution to the dual problems of carrying the dome's weight,
while preventing damage that could result from water leaking, freez-
ing, and thawing in severe Minnesota winters. Michelangelo's inspira-

tion could translate gracefully to the North Star State, but only with ingenious modifications.

Gilbert's clients expected all the amenities of the day. A press release from the architect's office boasted that "Among the many practical features are metal shelves, file cases and vault fixtures, comprehensive conduit work for installation of telephones, and an up-to-date heating plant."

Fireproofing was a must, with the loss of the first Capitol in flames still a fresh memory. Electric power was a new but reliable technology, which could be both functional and decorative. The Capitol was built with electric lights in offices, hallways, and state chambers, often in gilded sconces or crystal chandeliers. And the construction of the Renaissance-style statehouse was possible in large part because of the systems and techniques of nineteenth century industry: the steel mills that made the girders, the railroads that hauled the stone, and the steam hoists that lifted the pieces into place.

Just as the Capitol cloaked its up-to-date features in Renaissance stonework, it displayed *The Progress of the State* in antique dress. The sculpture group of that name is the main ornament of the Capitol façade, placed high above the entrance at the base of the dome. Commonly known as the Quadriga for its team of four horses abreast, the work represents a congratulatory view of Minnesota. The symbolism of the Quadriga is outlined by Julie C. Gauthier, a St. Paul painter and art teacher, who published *The Minnesota Capitol: Official Guide and History* with Gilbert's blessing in 1907:

> Standing upon a triumphal car drawn by four spirited horses, is the figure of "Prosperity," holding in one hand the horn of plenty, in the other a banner with the symbols of state. The horses are guided by two youthful women, full of life, strength and grace.

While the sentiment may be obscure to most visitors, the artistic effect is literally dazzling. Horses, figures, and chariot are made of sheet copper, with a gold leaf finish whose brilliance outshines the subtleties of the sculptors' art.

Gilbert engaged Daniel Chester French, one of the country's leading figure sculptors, for the Quadriga and stone figures on the façade below. A few years older than Gilbert and well experienced in monumental commissions, French is today best known for the huge seated figure in the Lincoln Memorial in Washington, D. C. Edward C. Potter, a specialist in animal sculpture, teamed with French to create the larger-than-life horses for the Quadriga. As its Latin name suggests, the Quadriga was a Roman artistic conceit. Americans adopted it as the crowning glory of triumphal arches like the one in Brooklyn's Grand Army Plaza, and many had seen French's earlier quadriga at Chicago's Columbian Exposition. There he had worked with Potter to create a sculpture group in which a statue of Columbus himself stood in the chariot.

Gilbert also turned to French for the six marble statues just below his Quadriga. According to the custom of the day, French did not carve the statues himself, any more than Gilbert himself built the Capitol stone by stone. The sculptor modeled them in clay at half their final size, and skilled stonecutters worked them up in marble on the Capitol grounds. The figures stand for "the six virtues that support and assist the progress of the state—the underlying virtues of good citizenship," as Gauthier explained them. *Bounty, Courage, Integrity, Prudence, Truth,* and *Wisdom:* four female and two male figures make up a cast of characters who symbolize rather than illustrate these strengths. The statues reflect conventional studio poses, and carry such typical studio equipment as *Truth's* mirror, *Prudence's* lamp, and the sword and shield of *Courage.* These fine points of iconology may be obscure to viewers so far below, but the statues add a graceful human accent and remind those entering the Capitol of the moral roots of their government. Capitol visitors actually see statues a generation further removed from Gilbert's models, for the six Virtues on the façade are replicas carved in the 1970s to replace the original marble figures, which had deteriorated from the effects of weather and pollution.

The Capitol's façade holds a wealth of smaller discoveries, too. Details carved in stone at every level enrich the marble surfaces. Many are common classical ornaments, like wreaths, swags, and medallions. Others have special meaning for Minnesota: a stately initial M within a laurel wreath, for instance, and robust carvings of the five-pointed star alluding to the state's motto, "L'Étoile du Nord," or North Star. Carved scroll or shell motifs enhance some moldings, such as those around the small circular windows of the dome. Evenly spaced across the façade, these details contribute to grand patterns under Minnesota's frequently changing skies. Bright sunlight etches crisp shadow patterns on the marble; overcast days soften the forms into shades of gray; snow and ice give the building a beard like a frosted giant.

The rest of the Capitol carries its classicism and craftsmanship as faithfully as the domed central mass. At either end of the main façade, columned pavilions of three-bay width press forward to balance the central loggia. Low copper-framed skylights, punctuated by flagpoles, rise to balance the dome. The visitor who takes a few extra minutes to stroll around the Capitol will better appreciate its fine points and its shortcomings. Turning at either corner, one sees that the sides of the building have their own two-story loggias with heroic columns, and equally generous granite stairways and terraces.

The north side of the Capitol has always suffered backhanded treatment. Gilbert's placement of the House of Representatives chamber here resulted in a truncated mass, which stands uncomfortably close to noisy, congested University Avenue. Here, too, the visitor inevitably finds automotive eyesores: coveted parking spaces for highly-placed officials and delivery entrances for contractors and supplies. But even these seem minor breaks in the stately rhythm of terraces, windows, and columns across the façade. One also finds here a tribute in stone to turn-of-the-century technology. A pair of carved medallions embellish the north façade above its central doors, featuring in one a steam locomotive speeding past telegraph wires, in the other an oceangoing steamship.

Compared to the white-bread blandness of the nearby Centennial or Transportation buildings from the 1950s, the Capitol is rich and filling fare. But a century ago, it was admired for its simplicity. One newspaper editorial praised the "severe simplicity of Gilbert's design, whose strength lies in the symmetry of its proportions and the subordination of all ideas of ornamental detail to the general effect of the mass." To turn-of-the-century eyes weary of frenetic Victorian revival styles, the Capitol's classicism appeared calm and consistent. A look at the runners-up in the Capitol competition illustrates the chosen design's relative modesty. Other entries featured numerous pediments, cupolas, and in one case, no less than eight smaller towers and domes about the main one.

Contemporaries also assessed Gilbert's statehouse by comparison to the World's Columbian Exposition of 1893. This great fair in Chicago introduced countless Americans to ideals of architecture and urban planning that re-shaped their towns and cities in the following decades. The fair set a standard for professional collaboration that Gilbert followed in building the Minnesota Capitol. Architects, sculptors, painters, and decorators—a catchall term for the skilled but often anonymous craftsmen who made acres of painted, carved, and gilded surfaces—worked together on the fair as a whole and on its individual buildings. Their goal was an aesthetic unity to which paintings and sculptures contributed their unique forms. But the architect was the boss: "commander-in-chief, leader, designer and creator of a whole," in the words of muralist Edwin H. Blashfield. Gilbert followed this precept in the Capitol and other monumental commissions for the rest of his career.

The buildings of the Columbian Exposition, with the notable exception of the Museum of Science and Industry (originally the fair's Fine Arts Building), lasted but a season. Made of a plaster and straw mix called staff on cast iron skeletons, the grandiose halls and sculpture groups burned or were otherwise destroyed at fair's end. But their classical style, imperial scale, and cosmopolitan boulevards became the reigning ideal for civic buildings. Gilbert submitted a design for a domed classical building to serve as the Minnesota pavilion. The commission went to Minneapolis architect William Channing Whitney's Renaissance palazzo design, but Gilbert brought home the lessons of the American Renaissance. He soon put them to work on a statehouse that remains one of that movement's landmarks. From the broad approaches that echo Gilbert's early landscaping plans to the small winged figure which greets the visitor at the front door, the Capitol is Minnesota's product of a local architect, a national movement, and an international tradition.

The Heart of the Capitol

$\mathcal{T}$HE CAPITOL'S fine marble façade promises equal splendors inside. Few visitors are disappointed. Entering this building begins an excursion through carefully staged spaces. The visitor steps from bright sunlight (or perhaps biting winds) into the shelter of a modest vestibule. Walls of a golden beige stone and panels painted deep red introduce an effect praised as "subdued splendor." Vaulted ceilings, alive with painted vines and blossoms, invite a closer look. But a glimpse of light from high overhead beckons the visitor a few steps further, into the heart of the Capitol, the 142-foot-high Rotunda.

Like the dome, the Rotunda marks the Capitol as a place for citizens to gather. The commissioners noted this essential feature:

> Canvass of public sentiment showed that a central dome and rotunda must be part of the design, and that the people would not be satisfied with any other. Moreover the rotunda, placed at the center of the building, provides space for the people who assemble on occasions of special public interest.

Gilbert set a star design into the Rotunda's polished stone floor. The star is made of thick cloudy glass, like slabs of ice from a northern lake, set in a brass framework. Ostensibly a light source for a meeting room below, the star also marks the epicenter of Minnesota's civic life.

Here in the Rotunda, tour groups gather to start their exploration of the Capitol. Officials read proclamations to their constituents, often under the eye of the television camera. Leaders of public life have lain in state in the Rotunda. On Sundays the space is often quiet, as hushed visitors study displays in glass cases. Spring days bring swarms of school-children, who fill the Rotunda with young voices. But for sheer aural overload, nothing can rival the occasional performance in the Rotunda of a chorus or a brass band.

The Rotunda can also echo with ominous notes. Reporter Burl Gilyard captured the mood at the end of a recent legislative session in the *Twin Cities Reader*:

Schoolchildren at the statue of William Colvill
in the Rotunda, circa 1985.

Walking into the Capitol on a sunny spring day, it takes your eyes a minute to adjust to the darkness of the hallways. You hear myriad faceless voices echoing throughout the building, ricocheting off the Rotunda from every angle. You can hear everything, but discern nothing—a perfect metaphor for shadowy politics.

The architect and commissioners were well aware that their Capitol would be the arena for debate, sometimes in its more acrimonious forms. They built the Capitol amid such wrangles: over cost-cutting versus lavish decor, over the use of fine marble versus the protection of home industries, over Twin Cities pomp versus outstate populism. Grand spaces like the Rotunda were their way of setting a stage on which citizens could act out the moment's triumphs or tragedies.

The North Star in the Rotunda floor marks the visitor's starting point, and provides a kind of compass, too. From this central point, the Capitol's symmetries unfold to the eyes, the mind, and the feet. The cross-shaped floor plan centering on the Rotunda, a time-honored way of organizing a building's spaces, orients the visitor to familiar directions of the compass. Entering the Rotunda from the south, one faces north to the wing that is home to the House of Representatives. To the east and west, grand staircases lead to the Supreme Court and Senate chambers. Symmetries of design and materials reinforce one's feeling of being well centered in the complex building. On the first floor, glass cases alternate with archways that give glimpses of corridors and stairways. One floor up, statues stand in niches between tall columns of polished Minnesota granite from Rockville and Ortonville. Higher still, ceiling decorations relate the Capitol to the cycle of seasons. Painted medallions in the upper corridors depict a seated woman with two children. A clockwise stroll leads the visitor from Winter in the north corridor, where the hooded woman holds her two infants; past Spring and Summer, with her growing children holding grains; to Autumn, in the west corridor, where the children help thresh the grains at her feet. This decorative orientation to space and time carries all the way to the dome, where symbols of the Zodiac circle high above the visitor's head, in twelve painted lunettes. A seven-foot-tall crystal chandelier, suspended high in the Rotunda, captivated a commentator in 1905:

> The great spherical electrolier, suspended from the center of the dome, lends a witchery of light to this interior in the early evening, when daylight and electricity strive for the mastery; when elusive vi-

olet shadows and golden reflections dance along the walls and play over the dome.

There is a rhythm to the Rotunda, a stately measure marked by the even pace of its arches and piers. This drumbeat of architectural cadence marks one's walk past relics of the Civil War. Beneath the first-floor arches are displays of war-torn regimental flags. Bronze plaques recount battles in a litany of place-names that touched the hearts of early visitors. One floor above are larger-than-life portrayals in bronze of Minnesota's Civil War leaders, whose exploits will later be seen in paintings that line the governor's formal chambers. For the Capitol is, among its other functions, a war memorial to the battles of its builders, men who had fought in the War Between the States and the Spanish-American War before entering public service in peacetime. Outside, the Quadriga and marble statues evoke abstract values; inside, sculptures, paintings, and plaques commemorate real-life sacrifices.

The Rotunda offers a feast of color and space. But as much as the interior finish embodies Gilbert's taste and talent, it also reflects political savvy. The architect and commissioners built a skillful case for making the Capitol's interior and grounds as majestic as its exterior. An appropriation of two million dollars was not enough to do the job—not in 1893, a time of national depression and low construction costs, and certainly not as costs and wages rose in the following years of construction. A speaker at the cornerstone-laying ceremony in 1898 hinted at the need for more money, as the commissioners "may be obliged to use ordinary wood work for interior finish and leave plain walls, unless the State in its wisdom make other provisions." The commissioners' 1901 report stated,

> This building is now so far along that the people of the state can see that they are to have, externally, one of the most beautiful and monumental public buildings in the United States. It should be finished in the interior in a suitable and permanent manner, and that finish should be better than what was originally planned.

A table of the costs and merits of capitols in seven other states showed that Minnesotans had already gotten more statehouse for less money. The commissioners pressed the need for a more generous building fund by listing the bleak prospects of a mere two-million-dollar Capitol: plain wood floors, plain plaster walls, "ordinary materials

*Chandelier in the dome lowered to the Rotunda floor
for repairs,* circa *1910.*

and workmanship." The list filled two dreary pages, followed by a proposal to spend another million dollars for "betterment of the original
design" and completion of exterior terraces, steps, and approaches.

The commissioners got their million, and two years later sought
$1,500,000 more. Gilbert enumerated artworks among the necessi-
ties for a modern Capitol, as important to the state as light and heat:

> The entire system of electrical equipment and operation has grown
> up within a few years, the installation of local telephones, call bells,
> heat control and other items of convenience have become practical
> necessities, and finally, in order to make a public building compare fa-
> vorably with others of modern construction and finish, it should be
> adorned with mural painting and sculpture of suitable character.

Despite strong opposition and a legislative investigation of the Board of State Capitol Commissioners, this request passed as well.

With a total budget of $4,500,000 at his disposal, Gilbert was eager to finish and furnish the Capitol. He marshaled a team of prominent painters to help him create "an effect of sumptuousness and subdued splendor," in muralist Cox's words. "This result is determined largely by the use of color, whether in the actual materials employed, the ornamental painting, or the introduction of mural decorations by our best artists." Gilbert harmonized these elements by selecting one basic type of stone for the interior walls, against which paintings and richer stone could be highlighted. He found suitable materials close at hand, to satisfy both political and artistic sensibilities. Minnesota quarries provided the limestone called Kasota stone. Honed to a subtle satin finish rather than polished to a high gloss, the stone has a color and character that defy verbal description. "Dull buff limestone with a pinkish tinge," Gauthier called it. "Grayish buff, with a golden tone," said Garnsey; Cox admired "the full warm tone of the yellow limestone." A magazine reporter wrote "The stone is the keynote of all the interior decoration. It has governed the selection of contrasting colours in the various marbles and other materials used, and with them has set the limits for the painters."

Gilbert's team of mural painters represented the highest levels of the art in America. All had contributed to the major projects of the American Renaissance movement: the Columbian Exposition of 1893, the Library of Congress, and celebrated civic buildings like Rhode Island's capitol and Baltimore's courthouse. John LaFarge, oldest of the painters by a generation, was esteemed for his experience and versatility in all the arts of decoration. Edwin H. Blashfield and Kenyon Cox were prolific writers, spokesmen as well as practitioners of the mural movement. Elmer E. Garnsey took on the key position of chief decorator for the Capitol interior. He had played that role in the Library of Congress, which had nineteen artists at work on 112 murals. Garnsey coordinated the work of decorators in all parts of Minnesota's statehouse, and also designed paintings for the legislative chambers and stair halls. But Gilbert, with commissioner Seabury's continual reminders, had to concern himself with costs as well as qualifications. Their correspondence reveals the business side of art. Gilbert studied the muralists' previous commissions to determine that "figure subjects by the best artists have averaged in cost from

$40 to $60 per square foot, and in one or two cases have cost $65." He persuaded LaFarge, Blashfield, and Garnsey to work at an average cost of $50 per square foot for Minnesota.

Elmer Garnsey came to Minnesota from his New York base in the summer of 1903, to study the building and propose his approach to its embellishment. He spelled out the didactic intent of the decoration to a St. Paul newspaper: "I believe that the Capitol will furnish . . . lessons in both patriotism and art, once it is complete." In the following months, Garnsey worked with Gilbert in St. Paul and New York to harmonize both the decorative scheme and the artistic temperaments at work for the Capitol. Commissioner Seabury pinpointed Garnsey's diplomatic mission:

> Mr. Garnsey has been with us, and met five of the seven members of our Board, and has also familiarized himself with the building and its surroundings, so that he can certainly help you to explain to the other gentlemen [artists] that this is not the 'wild and woolly West' that many people think it to be, but that our undertaking offers a splendid field for these noted artists, (whose names are, by no means, unknown to us here) . . .

Gilbert formed Garnsey, French, and other Capitol artists into a panel of advisors for artistic matters. His reports to the commissioners noted several meetings with the artists in New York, "mutually consulting and advising." The architect nonetheless felt it important to assert to Seabury his primacy in decorative decisions:

> I do not want to assume an undue share of credit myself in this matter, but I think it proper that you at least should know that I have personally directed Mr. Garnsey along certain definite lines of color, particularly in the rotunda, stairways and main corridors, and in the House Retiring Room. I do not say this to in any way belittle his own services, which are very great, but simply that I think history should be correctly written, in the statement that I have exercised a general direction of the color scheme as applied to the architecture in its main features, and exercised a critical function as to details, and that where I have not given instructions he and I have advised together.

Their success was best summarized by a critic who observed, "here is no building full of decorations but a noble building, fitly decorated."

Such a collaboration, necessarily executed at long distance, demanded a different approach than the Renaissance methods of fresco

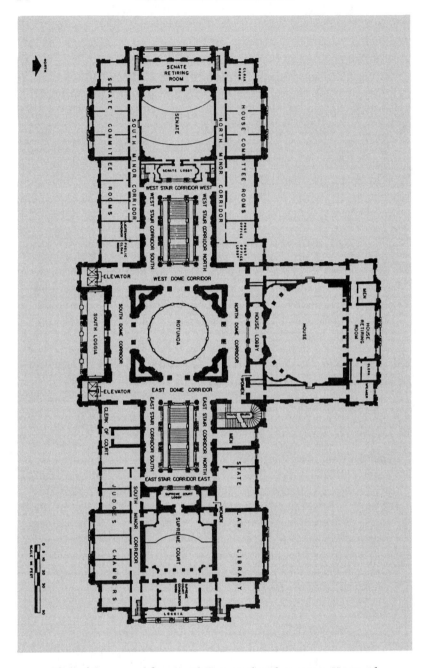

Plan of the second floor, with Senate chamber at top, House of Representatives chamber at right center, and Supreme Court at bottom.

painting. Gauthier's Capitol guidebook describes a key technical aspect of decorating the interior:

> Each painting was done upon a seamless canvas put upon a temporary stretcher, then taken off and rolled, to be shipped. Upon its arrival in St. Paul it was unrolled and smoothed over the curved surface of the wall, which had previously been given a thick coat of white lead to act as a gum or paste. The canvas was put on and off many times before it went on properly, and each time the creases were smoothed out as in mounting a photograph.

Gauthier's summary applauds the convenience of this modern mural technique; but a visitor to the Capitol can easily imagine the tedious labor of mounting thousands of square feet of murals, on scaffolds high above the floor.

Gilbert and Garnsey thus coordinated the general decoration with the work of several distant artists chosen to "appropriately represent the growth and progress of the Northwest" in paint. The Capitol guidebook spelled out the challenge: "The artists were advised that although the subjects would probably have to be treated allegorically, care must be taken not to fill the building with Greek gods and goddesses, as these were considered inappropriate for a building devoted to the transaction of business." American muralists faced this conundrum wherever building commissioners sought to enlist their art in the service of both universal truths and local pride. They made fine distinctions between the "ornamental" painting that embellished an architectural setting, "pictorial" subjects that aimed to recount historic events in America's past, and "decorations" that would personify civic virtues—usually in classical dress (or undress). The word "decoration" may call to the visitor's mind a modest, even frivolous garnish today. But allied to the names of leading artists like LaFarge, Blashfield, or John Singer Sargent (who declined Gilbert's invitation to paint the Rotunda, due to previous commitments), a decoration was a figure painting of heroic scale that would ennoble any building. The visitor to Minnesota's statehouse has only to look up in the Rotunda and stair halls to see how Gilbert and his artists met the challenge.

The Rotunda walls hold a cycle of four paintings called *The Civilization of the Northwest*, a broad theme proposed by the artist and approved by the architect and Board. In artist Edward E. Simmons' treatment, this is no plain saga of settler families breaking the sod.

Simmons rendered his theme with an intellectual detachment that matched his physical distance from Minnesota. Working in his Paris studio, he composed an allegory of floating figures and grand gestures. His colors harmonize beautifully with the Rotunda, thanks in part to Gilbert's foresight. The architect sent stone samples to Paris so that Simmons could adjust his palette to the colors that would surround the paintings. Simmons' compositions ingeniously fill the spandrels, or trapezoidal spaces between the arches in the Rotunda. But the literal-minded viewer, expecting to learn of Minnesota's heritage, may well find these pictures obscure or just silly. The four scenes depict a young man leaving home, clearing land, and finally enthroned amid symbols of prosperity (including a model of a domed building like Minnesota's statehouse).

Following the pictorial conventions of the American Renaissance, Simmons painted his westering youth, a symbol of "brave American spirit," in an allegorical Never-Never Land. Gauthier's guidebook offers a painting-by-painting glossary of the symbolism. One passage will suffice to render the artspeak of the day:

> The third panel is particularly interesting. It represents the man, no longer a youth, breaking the soil by removing an immense boulder which bears crystals and gold. 'Hope' and 'Wisdom' [two female figures in flowing draperies] are still with him. From the broken soil have sprung figures bearing maize and flowers. A woman with a child indicates fertility. All bear upon the idea of agriculture.

Simmons recalled the commission as "one of the largest orders I ever received." But he also left a wry tale of the hazards of allegory in his 1922 autobiography *From Seven to Seventy*.

> There were several guides in the Capitol employed to show the visitors around and explain the sights to them. I thought it would be splendid for me to give them special instructions about my work, so that they would not make the usual ludicrous mistakes. But guides seem to be a different breed of animal chosen for the wide range of their imaginations. I supposed everything was going all right, when one day a particularly loquacious one came up to me and showed me a miniature palette in his buttonhole, telling me he was an artist himself and belonged to a club of artists. He knew all about the ladies in my decoration—the one veiled in chiffon (which I had made for Hope) he called Sin, entirely neglecting the nude woman in the fore-

ground, Sin, clinging to a grizzly. He had probably received his early education in and about a Burlesque show.

Further indignities awaited Simmons' work. The mural made headlines again in 1912: "$10,000 Painting Falls from Dome." Wisdom, Hope, and the "brave American spirit" fell a hundred feet to the Rotunda floor on a 94 degree September day; a month later a second panel fell. Glued back in place, they remained for another three-quarters of a century. In 1985, sharp-eyed workers in the Capitol noticed a section of the canvas tearing loose. But prompt restoration work saved Simmons' hero from another fall.

A few steps from the Rotunda bring visitors to similarly grand spaces. More than just passageways, the stair halls offer as rich an experience as the Rotunda itself. "Other states have their dome-bedecked Capitols, and some boast interiors of no small grandeur," exclaims a 1981 guide to American architecture, "but it is doubtful if any can equal the Roman-bath splendor of the upper halls and grand stairways of this one in Minnesota." Generous spaces, a carefully orchestrated variety of materials, and paintings by prominent muralists make the stair halls worth a thoughtful stroll—though they also serve to move large tour groups or busy pages through the Capitol.

These spaces are Gilbert's showcase of precious stones. Here he found more latitude for exotic materials, for his extensive use of Kasota stone had appeased local opinion. The stairways themselves are made of polished Hauteville marble that closely matches the Kasota stone walls; jewel-like marble insets add a wealth of color and pattern. *The Craftsman* magazine enumerated the new Capitol's attractions in 1905: "The great staircases of the Rotunda are resplendent with marbles—Hauteville and Echaillon from France, Skyros from Greece, and Old Convent Siena and Breche Violette from Italy." Garnsey, too, admired their "highly polished surfaces sufficiently splendid for a king's palace, none too magnificent for the Capitol of a sovereign American state."

Prudent use of his quarter-million dollar art budget allowed Gilbert to commission Kenyon Cox and Henry Oliver Walker to paint decorations for each skylit stair hall. Here again, the orientation by theme and direction sets the stage for the chambers the visitor will see on the second floor. For the east stair hall leading to the Supreme Court, Cox painted *The Contemplative Spirit of the East* as a trio of

West stair hall with Henry O. Walker's lunette,
Yesterday, Today and Tomorrow *(at center), and painted figures*
representing Minnesota industries at left and right.

women in classical draperies. "The composition as a whole is meant
to form a fitting introduction to the decorations of the Supreme
Court, which depict the development of Law," the artist wrote. Cox
locked his composition firmly into its architectural setting with a muralist's sleight of hand: the figures sit on a bench painted to match the
color and lines of the Kasota stone architrave. His winged central figure is angel, madonna, and *Thinker* all in one. "Her pose and expression of face indicate deep study," Gauthier noted. To her right sits
"Letters," open book at hand. "Law," at her left, holds a bridle and
staff, symbols of restraint that the visitor may have noted on French's
Quadriga; and she sits next to a stone tablet that hints at LaFarge's
lunette of Moses in the courtroom ahead.

For the stair hall to the west, Walker conceived an allegory of "the
transmission of knowledge and the forces of civilization across the
ages," a theme his contemporaries identified with the westward

spread of America's population. Gilbert himself described it to the Commissioners: "A figure of Old Age bending over and conserving the embers of the fire of knowledge, passes the flame on to Maturity who in turn ignites or lights the torch of Youth, illustrating poetically the idea of the progress that is supposed to be typical of the West gaining knowledge from the past and transmitting it to the future." This mural, too, calls to mind symbolism seen outside: the lamp held by French's *Prudence*. It also celebrates the nineteenth century woman's role as society's chosen keeper of the flame of culture and learning. Walker titled the actresses of his drama by their Latin names, in one of the Capitol's few word-for-word borrowings from Rome: Cras (yesterday), Hodie (today), and Hera (tomorrow).

Twelve smaller lunettes attempt a more down-to-earth interpretation of Minnesota life. Each depicts an occupation or industry, such as logging, mining, or farming, as a hard-working man or woman. Garnsey designed the lunettes, each with its figure filling the semicircular space on a dramatic scale. His assistant Arthur R. Willett painted them, in a common division of labor for turn-of-the-century mural projects. A pleasant landscape background unifies the twelve scenes, but they are a decidedly mixed dozen in concept. Some suggest their themes convincingly. *Winnowing* is a plausible farm woman, and *Mining* a laborer who wields a serviceable-looking wrench. *Stonecutting* is so specific to its setting that a corner of the Capitol itself forms the workman's backdrop. But Garnsey resorted to allegorical stand-ins for some subjects. Commerce and milling, for example, are symbolized by women whose antique draperies are a poor fit with the locomotive and mill behind them. In art, as in politics, the ideal and the real jostle each other in the statehouse halls.

Not all the elements of the Capitol are so grand or grandiose. Many modest features serve to unify the corridors and delight the visitor. One can take a Capitol tour as a vicarious nature walk, in search of the state's flora and fauna rendered into art. Long lines of stenciled motifs link strong colors with more subtle hues, well summarized in Gauthier's guidebook: "The vaulted ceilings of the first floor are decorated with bands, circles, and rectangles of grains and fruits native to Minnesota . . . while panels of blue and violet, complementary to the prevailing color, prevent a tiresome monotony." The attentive visitor can trace certain colors and motifs all along the halls. Sheaves of grain, cornucopias spilling out fruits, and bouquets of the state flower embellish the first floor. The halls one floor above are painted with long chains of corn, shocks of wheat, and heaps of vegetables. "The decoration is kept simple and with no modeling, and ornaments the surface without disturbing its flatness," noted Gauthier in appreciation of a technique that narrowly escapes kitsch. Oak leaves and acorns appear everywhere, as stenciled filigree on red and brown panels, or as deeply sculpted and gilded moldings around skylights. Garnsey completed his work long before the Minnesota legislature consecrated a host of state symbols, so the visitor will look in vain for the state mushroom (the morel), the state grain (wild rice), or the state muffin (blueberry) among the stenciled designs.

The animal kingdom is also present in the Capitol, where eagles are the preeminent species. They appear in painted form, on two of Garnsey's figure compositions in third floor halls. They spread their wings in high relief from the bronze Rotunda railings at the same level. Eagles are cast in the bases of tall bronze light posts in the corridors, and they hover in a leaded glass skylight above the elegant spiral staircase at the northeast angle of the building. The national bird shares the Rotunda with Minnesota's state mammal. The gopher, or thirteen-striped ground squirrel, appears in heraldic pairings on the bronze railings of the third floor. Gophers, loons, and lady's-slippers also enliven the bronze gates at the entrances to the Senate, House of Representatives, and Supreme Court chambers.

In motifs great and small, the interior decoration blends classical antiquity and Renaissance conventions with a Minnesota idiom. The capitals that top dozens of stone columns and pilasters, inside and out, epitomize this vernacular touch. These stone or painted plaster capitals show the deeply-cut acanthus leaves typical of the Corinthian order: but in this statehouse, they also sprout the stylized leaves and blossoms of the pink and white lady's-slipper, a wild orchid found deep in Minnesota forests. Thus Nature, stylized by the decorator's touch, stays eternally fresh in the art of the Capitol.

Gilbert and Seabury realized that the statehouse they had labored a dozen years to build was left incomplete. Early photographs published in art magazines have an eerie emptiness. The only human presence to be seen is a guard on duty at the front door, and a spittoon on the landing of one grand staircase. The Board's final report suggested opportunities for future generations to enliven the halls, with "statues of men prominent in the history of our State, for niches

Rotunda capital with lady's-slipper motif.

inside the building." Since that time, only about twenty statues and plaques have been placed. They reflect Minnesotans' changing conceptions of what (and who) matters, from Civil War heroes to civil rights leaders.

Bronze statues of four Civil War officers—William Colvill, John B. Sanborn, James Shields, and Alexander Wilkin—hold commanding positions in the Rotunda's stone niches. As portraits of real people who made substantial contributions to their state and country, these grizzled soldiers balance the lightweights of Simmons' murals overhead. All stand larger than life in the uniforms of their Minnesota regiments, their haughty scale and military stance in striking contrast to the motley crowds in the halls. The Wilkin and Sanborn statues are the work of John Karl Daniels, a Norwegian-born Minnesota sculptor whose figures can be seen on the Capitol grounds and across the state. Shields was modeled by Chicago sculptor Frederick C. Hibbard, and Catherine Backus of Minneapolis created the statue of Colvill.

While the statues are likely to impress the Capitol visitor with their air of authority and tradition, Gilbert was not pleased with them. He recommended selecting a sculptor of international reputation for the Colvill memorial, and withheld his blessing from the citizens group that commissioned Mrs. Backus in 1908. "My advice in this respect has been ignored," he wrote to the group's chairman, "and you now have before you models for this important work by persons who are naturally ambitious but who, so far as I can ascertain, utterly lack the training and experience to execute the work. You would not employ a foreman in your factory upon such principles." Gilbert was less restrained in a handwritten note to his St. Paul office:

> What I think they want, is my 'for nothing advice,' and to say to the public that they acted only under my advice, and make me responsible for a damned bad statue, which they have not the nerve, nor the sense to accept or reject by themselves. . . They shall not mar that building with my concurrence.

But Gilbert's drive to control all aspects of the Capitol, inside and out, was unable to restrain Minnesotans' zeal for memorials. Backus' Colvill statue was placed in the Capitol, and other memorials soon followed.

Bronze plaques sculpted in low relief commemorate people and events on the Rotunda walls. A classic art form that flourished in the hands of only a few American sculptors when the Capitol was new, the *bas-relief* has since become a staple of Hall of Fame likenesses. Plaques in the Rotunda strive for both pictorial and didactic effect. Backus designed a bronze tablet *In Memory of the First Minnesota Volunteer Infantry.* The plaque features a lengthy account of the regiment's actions, including its heroic charge at Gettysburg. Flanking this text are insipid portraits of the First Minnesota's five colonels, and a woman accompanying a flag-bearing boy. War widow or allegory of Victory? The figure suggests both, with more feeling than the five colonels combined. St. Paul's Brioschi Studios created an even busier memorial to veterans of the Spanish-American War. It combines in a dozen square feet lengthy inscriptions, medallions of politicians, Renaissance river gods, an *alto-relievo* eagle, and fullblown scenes of land and sea battles, all enframed in a border of lady's-slippers.

Other plaques offer a lesson in American history, and honor two

Minnesota women. The Northwest Ordinance of 1787, a federal statute that triggered the country's westward expansion, is honored on a bronze tablet placed after its 150th anniversary. Allegory was out of fashion by 1938. Instead, expansionist rhetoric and a map of the lands that became the Midwest tell the tale of "the Old Northwest Territory, the First Colony of the United States." Two portrait plaques nearby signify another kind of expansion: a broadening of Minnesota's recognition of rights and deeds. Side by side with memorials to fighting men hang likenesses of Martha G. Ripley and Clara H. Ueland. Dr. Ripley's plaque, designed by Minneapolis sculptor Charles S. Wells, pays tribute to "the Pioneer Woman Physician" who founded a maternity hospital in Minneapolis: "She served humanity." The Ueland tablet by Louise Cross mixes portraiture with platitudes. "As she fought ever, without malice and without hatred, so may we fight," the plaque advises. Yet it offers no facts of Ueland's field of battle, the drive for women's suffrage in her state. More ironic still is her identification only by her married name, as "Mrs. Andreas Ueland."

Portrait busts in marble, bronze, and painted plaster stand witness throughout the first floor. An elegantly simple bust of Cass Gilbert by Edmond Quinn bears no identification beyond a name, for Gilbert's work is visible everywhere in the Capitol. At the foot of the stairs to the Senate, one finds busts of two men who served with distinction in Minnesota's political life: Hubert H. Humphrey (by George M. Bassett) and Nicholas D. Coleman (by Paul T. Granlund). A bust of Ignatius Donnelly, nineteenth century maverick politico and man of letters (sculpted by Daniels), faces Bassett's bust of twentieth century conservationist and author Sigurd F. Olson across the north corridor. And to the east of the Rotunda, bronzes placed in the 1980s honor two men for their own lives, and also as representatives of people of color who had long been ignored among Capitol tributes: Dakota Indian leader Wabasha III (by JoAnne Bird), and "seeker of peace, justice, and truth" Rev. Dr. Martin Luther King Jr. (by Bassett).

Few in number, narrow in range, the busts and plaques in the Capitol are more like a casual head count than a roll call of the powerful and famous. Perhaps the notoriously modest citizens of the Gopher State have found the Capitol too finished to improve. But one who wonders if statues could match Gilbert's conceits by size alone need only walk to the northernmost corner of the first floor. Just inside the doors to University Avenue, Albert Jaegers' *German Pio-*

neers are frozen in mid-stride. This sculpture group is the plaster model for a 1920 monument to colonial settlers in Germantown, Pennsylvania. Presented in 1959, the sculpture was placed in the Capitol by Minnesota's German-Americans, at a time when statehood centennial celebrations led several ethnic groups to mark their contributions through art. Jaegers' seven-foot-tall couple in seventeenth century dress, rushing toward a blank wall, presents a case study in the need for careful placement that respects the interplay of art and architecture. The Capitol interior, designed for a sensual and intellectual unity, can render carelessly placed additions trivial or crude. But it also offers stunning lessons in the orchestration of grand, sumptuous spaces, awaiting the visitor at the top of the marble stairs.

The Minnesota State Capitol.

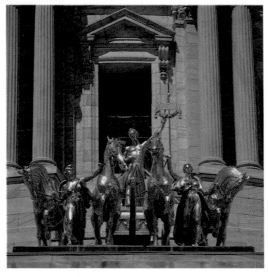

The Progress of the State, *known as The Quadriga.*

The Capitol Grounds in Autumn.

The Capitol Rotunda.

The Capitol Rotunda.

The East Stair Hall.

The House of Representatives Chamber.

Looking up into the Capitol Dome.

The Governor's Reception Room.

The Rotunda floor, with North Star Symbol.

The Senate Chamber.

The Supreme Court Chamber.

Ceiling and Skylight, House of Representatives Chamber.

Eagle at the base of the Capitol dome.

View of St. Paul from the Capitol roof.

Fireworks on Independence Day.

Three Grand Chambers

A WALK THROUGH the forest of marble columns on the Capitol's second floor is an exploration of ideas about art and government. The textbook concept of balance of powers here finds expression in the symmetry of Gilbert's floor plan. Tradition and precedent—the "love of permanence and continuity" that Kenyon Cox espoused—is apparent in stenciled slogans and painted figures. Here one finds paintings that aim to teach civic virtues, and ideas lettered in gold to ornament the walls. Elmer Garnsey called this "the grand floor of the Capitol." Here are its three largest spaces, equaling the Rotunda for richness of materials and elegance of design. Gilbert gave distinct personalities to the chambers of the Senate, the House of Representatives, and the Supreme Court. There are elements common to all. Each has its skylight, its great arching surfaces enriched with decorative paintings, and its mahogany furnishings. Each has a formality appropriate to the disciplines of making, debating, and interpreting Minnesota's laws. Like stage sets for the dramas of civic life, these three chambers urge a sense of dignity upon those who enter.

A convincing testimony to the success of these spaces is the fact that the Senate, House, and Court have all respected and preserved the original designs of their chambers. They have housed their increased numbers and state-of-the-art hardware within Gilbert's design. Each chamber has seen its surface changes and remodelings, sometimes with wholesale redecorating of carpets, paint colors, and wall treatments. But surprisingly often, walls were repainted to duplicate original colors and patterns—even though the time-consuming process was costly, and the original colors out of fashion at the time of remodeling. A revived interest and appreciation of turn-of-the-century art during the 1980s brought the keepers of the Capitol back to Gilbert's basics. Realizing that a piecemeal approach to restoration was likely to perpetuate errors, the Minnesota Historical Society, the Capitol Area Architectural and Planning Board, and Miller-Dunwiddie Associates, Inc. made careful studies of the voluminous records of the

Supreme Court chamber, looking west to LaFarge's Socrates mural,
circa 1913.

building of the Capitol, inventoried physical conditions and uses, and
tabulated the changes each space in the building had undergone
since 1905. Historical Society staff members identified original Capitol furniture. Some pieces were still where the original users put
them, some were out of the building or even out of the county. The
Senate and the House restored their chambers in 1988 and 1989–90,
respectively, with an attention to detail that the demanding Gilbert

would have appreciated. Ongoing restorations of other public spaces take the architect's documented intentions as a guiding rule.

The functions of each chamber are matters of regulation and custom. As early as its first competition in 1894, the Board of State Capitol Commissioners had spelled out the number of legislators, judges, and other officials the new statehouse was to accommodate. Gilbert satisfied and went well beyond these requirements. He enhanced the spirit of each chamber with pictorial allegories and well-chosen inscriptions.

The visitor enters the Supreme Court below an aphorism of nineteenth century orator Daniel Webster, that leaves no doubt about the high ideals for this room: "Justice is the great interest of man on earth. It is the ligament which holds civilized nations together. Wherever her temple stands and so long as it is duly honored, there is a foundation for social security, general happiness, and the improvement and progress of our race." A small vestibule frames the first view of the court. In a niche at one's left is a bronze bust of Warren E. Burger, Minnesota native and former chief justice of the United States Supreme Court. The 1984 bust, by Walker Hancock, offers a silent welcome and a reminder of Minnesota's contribution to the national judiciary.

Stepping into the Court chamber, one enters a zone of hushed restraint, "severely dignified and richly, though simply, furnished," as Gauthier put it. Every element has its well-defined place, marking each person's role: square-backed chairs for the justices, tables for the litigants in a generously open space before the rostrum, and a span of benches for visitors and spectators. A polished mahogany balustrade marks the boundary between the high court's participants and those who come to witness the proceedings. Colors and forms reflect the clarity that citizens seek here. The room is square in plan, with broad arches that lift one's eyes to the domed ceiling. In strong contrast to the sensual effects of stones, colors, and patterns in the halls outside, the Court chamber is all smooth surfaces of white marble, blue paint, and gold leaf. Gilded panels brighten the dome's surface, while painted wreaths encircle the word "LEX" in each gilded spandrel. The design takes its effect from the gravity of plain, well-ordered surfaces, arrayed as logically as the leatherbound law books behind the judges. But the chamber's most profound elements, artistically and philosophically, are John LaFarge's murals.

Nearly seventy years old when he accepted this commission, La-Farge was the acknowledged master of American mural painting. He chose "more novel or less used themes," he told Gilbert in 1903, "so that your building would have an additional mark of special choice and care by the avoidance of the commonplace." LaFarge looked to world history for four key moments in the development of law. In this search he enjoyed the advice of a remarkable circle of friends. He told Gilbert that his pictorial concepts were shaped by conversations with historian Henry Adams, secretary of state John M. Hay, and United States senator Henry Cabot Lodge, a choice gathering of America's social and intellectual elite. The four lunettes were applauded from the beginning as more imaginative than merely historical, more decorative than illustrational—qualities that ranked them high in the mindset of the American Renaissance movement. "They have a singularly appropriate suggestion for a law chamber," the correspondent of *International Studio* magazine noted in 1905, "while enforcing an historical sequence of facts rather than a group of abstractions, and in execution are worthily the latest work of a master artist."

LaFarge composed his scenes from the Old Testament, classical Greece, ancient China, and the Middle Ages. In each lunette, several figures in carefully researched costume act their parts in convincing settings. Each scene has a message about the long tradition of law in which twentieth-century citizens participate here. *The Moral and Divine Law,* facing the entrance, shows Moses on Mount Sinai receiving the word of God. "The scene is said to portray the terrifying silence where a low-spoken word awakens strange echoes," noted Gauthier. LaFarge sought to instill awe with his eerie depiction of Moses kneeling at the apex of the composition. The prophet's son Joshua hushes onlookers, both the unseen Israelites implied by the picture's action, and visitors entering the chamber in real time. In the north lunette, Confucius and his followers enact *The Recording of Precedents.* The Chinese sage is seated before a landscape that the widely-traveled La-Farge assured his clients was as accurate as the costumes. "I happen to have read and to know a great deal more than most Western men about these matters," he wrote to Seabury. The artist's published writings and masterful watercolors bear out his boasts.

Greek philosophers debate *The Relation of the Individual to the State* on the west wall. Its placement above the entrance to the courtroom keeps the image and method of Socrates before the eyes of the

Justices' Consultation Room, circa *1913.*

justices who sit opposite the lunette. Here again the artist's antiquarian research is evident in the period costumes and the exedra, or semicircular terrace, which extends the arch form of the lunette into the picture's space. An approaching chariot recalls the Quadriga on the Capitol façade, while lush flowers in one corner demonstrate another aspect of LaFarge's fame. "He is a much admired writer and lecturer on the subject of art," gushed Gauthier, "yet he delights in painting flowers!" The fourth lunette illustrates *The Adjustment of Conflicting Interests* in a medieval episode. Raymond, count of Toulouse, takes an oath before the bishop and magistrate of his city. LaFarge composed this meeting of church and state with all the scholar's resources at hand: "Hundreds of books and engravings and

photographs have been consulted or purchased as above for this purpose." His attention to detail is obvious in the dress of count and
bishop, while the mural's architectural setting displays a precedent to
the Minnesota courtroom in its classical details. The painting's frozen
gestures of decorum present yet another cue for Minnesotans who
hear, try, or witness cases here.

LaFarge's mural cycle is the end product of his research and in-
vention, but also of disputes that nearly led the painter and his clients
into court themselves. While LaFarge was painting Socrates and Confucius for the Capitol, he was also trading acerbic letters with Gilbert
and Seabury over the mural contract. The architect and commissioners expected substantial drawings and color studies from LaFarge. He
in turn railed at the Board's provincialism and sought payments that
Seabury thought unearned. Their spat bequeathed to history not just
a glimpse of the mundane matters that underlay an art of noble sentiment, but a lengthy letter dated July 16, 1904, in which the artist
spelled out to Seabury his working methods. LaFarge's patronizing
discourse gives insight into the muralist's process: the research in
books and pictures, the purchase of costumes and accessories, the
hiring of skilled assistants, the projection of drawings onto canvas
with photographic slides, and finally the painting of the canvas in oils
by the master and his crew. "With these explanations you can see
how wrong it would be for me to skimp this work or make it inaccu-
rate at the risk of further errors and consequent indefinite delay," he
concluded. "I can call myself one of the principal experts in the country and I know that my method is the best and in fact the only one
susceptible of carrying out the work on such a scale."

Seabury responded just as firmly, telling the artist "you should
just drop all this contentious spirit, and go ahead with your individual
work." The melodrama peaked in a New York gallery where Gilbert
viewed LaFarge's work, snubbing the peevish artist with a minimal
acknowledgment. After private discussions through intermediaries,
all parties agreed to terms for the completion of the commission.

The Moses mural has been modified: a doorway around which the
lunette had been installed was enclosed and painted to blend into the
composition, probably in the 1930s. Late twentieth century visitors
also experience the courtroom in a different palette than Gilbert and
Garnsey intended. In their original scheme, St. Paul artist Cleora
Wheeler wrote, "red velvet hangings tone in with the deep rich colors

of the canvases." The pale ivory panels and solid blue carpet that replaced those red fabrics in the 1970s cool down the courtroom, but
its marble, gilding, and mahogany furnishings remain. The courtroom
has housed a judiciary that itself made history in 1991. In that year it
became the first state supreme court to have a majority of women justices—a milestone of women's long twentieth century progress from
symbolic presence, as in Cox's mural, to public office.

Two doors at the back of the chamber lead into the Justices' Consultation Room, a space with rich associations that afforded Gilbert
an exercise in Colonial Revival design. It is "a copy, except in propor-
tion, of the Supreme Court in Independence Hall in Philadelphia
where the Declaration of Independence was signed," Gauthier noted.
"Its pure white woodwork and marble mantle-pieces, gold-framed
portraits, and mahogany chairs are simple and restful." The justices
had offices along an adjoining corridor, until moving into the Minnesota Judicial Center in 1991.

Gilbert's concern for creating a total environment is evident in his
designs for furniture for offices, as well as for public spaces. Existing
drawings and specifications document the styles of furniture, but his
correspondence brings the process to life. Among the many occupants of the new Capitol who sought the architect's special attention,
Judge Edwin W. Jaggard was most specific and delightfully candid in
his requests. "Another matter concerns the much debated problem of
a lounge," he wrote Gilbert in January, 1905. "I would like to have a
moderately comfortable plain one; not as hard as the Secretary of
State has. That is stately but inadequate for my too too solid and
ample frame. It does well to sit on but is ill adapted to balmy sleep."
Gilbert's sketch for such a lounge, upholstered in leather, is still
clipped to the judge's letters.

Leaving the Court chamber, visitors find a long vista framed by
ranks of marble columns. The view extends through the Rotunda and,
as if seen in a mirror, doubles down the west stair hall to the door of
the Senate chamber. Elmer Garnsey wrote with pride of "the most
splendid character" of this artfully framed view: "The atmosphere is
golden in tone, ranging from the dull ochres in the stone below to the
gilded capitols above" and culminating in "the sumptuous color of
painted decorations." He also disclosed a colorist's trick of manipulat-
ing natural light, somewhat as a photographer uses colored filters.
The stair hall skylights are tinted with "slightly amber glass, giving a

delicate tone to the light that floods the spaces, mellowing and uniting the effect." Like many of the Capitol's subtleties of interior lighting, this effect is today garbled by 1970s fixtures that throw strong light upward from the cornice. These modern fixtures are easily identified by their bland functional casings. No designer of Gilbert's day would resist the temptation to encrust them with gilt ornament. They satisfy the late twentieth century's urge to splash bright light on every indoor surface, however illogical it is to beam it up toward a skylight. But the ambience the original designers worked carefully to create is bleached out in the process.

The letter of the law follows the visitor out of the courtroom, in gilded panels high on the second floor walls. There, quotations in Roman capital letters offer meditations on law and justice. These red-letter inscriptions come "mostly from the utterances of men who have passed into history," Gauthier reported, "and added to these are a few strong words from Minnesota men who have achieved national fame." Citizens thus walk the halls with Justinian, Abraham Lincoln, and St. Paul's Archbishop John Ireland, whose words link twentieth century Minnesota to the minds of centuries past.

The modern stomach is evident in the corridors, too. Vending machines, plastic garbage cans, and a prosaic metal lunch counter stand in the light of the tall French windows of the south corridor. Gilbert's palette of "Pompeian red, with borders in ivory and yellow" competes with hues of ketchup and mustard in this corridor dubbed "Ulcer Gulch." Here legislators and lobbyists do some fast-food politicking during brief recesses. Though the legislative session lasts only five months, the portable fixtures of "Ulcer Gulch" remain in place year 'round, a tribute to shortsighted habit. But the snack bar does have its aesthetic uses. Minnesotans who question whether their statehouse is worth maintaining and restoring can see one alternative right here. Imitation wood-grain contact papers and faux-granite finishes cannot ennoble plastic furnishings; nor do they seriously injure the Capitol's dignity. The contrast between Rockville granite columns and plastic trashpails can help citizens appreciate how splendid their statehouse still is, after almost a century of use.

Cass Gilbert's intentions for Capitol furniture are better seen in the oak benches he placed through the halls. The detail-haunted architect did not leave furnishing choices to chance or whim. His letters reveal that Gilbert even sought special colors and finishes for

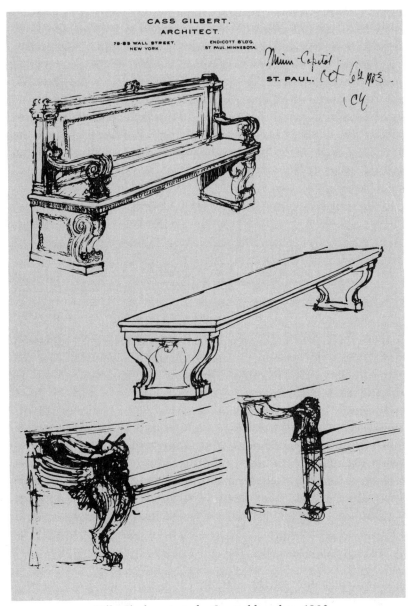

Gilbert's drawings for Capitol benches, 1903.

metal switchplates and rubber spittoons, to harmonize those essentials with his grand scheme. He made drawings and specifications for seventy-four varieties of tables, chairs, desks, and other furnishings. Pieces like the Supreme Court's testimonial table are one of a kind, while standard styles were ordered by the dozens or even hundreds. Herter Brothers, a leading New York furniture and interior decoration firm of the American Renaissance movement, was awarded the contract for furniture. The firm produced many of the special order pieces, while subcontracting other unique items and many of the standard styles to companies in New York, Minnesota, and other states. The hallway benches are Gilbert designs that Capitol visitors can use freely (even for a lunch break). Built of substantial oak slabs, the benches have carved leaf and scroll motifs, with contrasting wood inlays. The "WY Settees," as specifications denote fourteen white oak benches for the first floor halls, have plain, flat backs and arms. Eight "WX Settees" on the second floor are made of English oak with more richly carved backs, open arms, and Ionic details that echo in miniature the classical order seen in second floor chambers. From the comfort of a bench in the west corridor, the visitor can read more red-on-gold inscriptions high on the wall. Here the words of George Washington, Daniel Webster, and others invite one to meditate on liberty and government, before entering the Senate chamber.

America's largest state senate convenes in this chamber at the Capitol's west end. Visitors can "meet" the sixty-seven senators electronically, on a video program in the vestibule that gives facts and figures at the touch of a finger. From this point forward, the chamber looks much as it did when the sixty-three men who made up the 1905 senate first took their seats here. "The Senate Chamber is a square room finished in French Fleur de Peche marble, with its creamy ground and violet coloring," *The Craftsman* magazine reported. "The furniture is mahogany and the leading colors in the decorations are ivory and gold with some old blue." This much is evident to a visitor today, who may only see the chamber through a bronze gate cast with gophers and lady's-slippers. Perhaps it is this vantage point, from outside looking in, that gives the room its regal air. But the presiding officer's throne-like dais, aligned with the view back to the Supreme Court, is enough to introduce an opulence that bespeaks authority. The visitor who gains entrance to the Senate floor will best appreciate

The Minnesota Senate in session, 1943.

how lavishly this space houses what one observer called "the greatest club in Minnesota."

The Senate Chamber exemplifies that ideal of collaboration that the American Renaissance movement loved. Garnsey, modest about his own hand in the work, explained how the multitude of elements were orchestrated: "There is a subdued richness of color and tone in this room, which has been accomplished by the association of several artists, whose purpose has been to achieve a harmonious result, rather than the exploitation of the individual." Gilbert's progress reports to the Board bear this out. His accounts of meetings in New York show the architect's delight in his teamwork with Garnsey and Blashfield. The arts of the painter, carver, gilder, cabinetmaker, stonecutter and muralist all contribute to this chamber.

Gilbert's experience with marble for the Senate room illustrates the uncertainties of his worldwide hunt for the right materials. He had planned to use a different stone entirely. "I wanted to get the Tres Boukes [marble] on account of a certain golden color which runs through it and because it was a more unusual marble," he wrote to his occasional hunting partner Seabury. "I have found by experience that all these special marbles are about as difficult to count on as a flight of ducks over a duck pass." The gaudy violet of the Fleur de Peche (peach blossom) stone set the palette for wall panels painted a soft rose color. A rich blue, patterned with gold leaf, provided the backdrop for the Senate leader's desk and chair, which are carved with eagles, a bold five-point star, and the motto "L'Étoile du Nord." Gold-on-blue patterns line the niches at all four corners of the chamber, in each of which a United States senator from Minnesota is portrayed in a bust of white marble. Senators Cushman K. Davis, Knute Nelson, Henry M. Rice, and William D. Washburn thus appear in the noble material employed in imperial times for the senators of Rome. The gold-on-blue treatment continues in "an inscription in gold in which the lettering counts as an ornament, filling the entire width of the frieze," in Garnsey's description. The words come once more from Daniel Webster:

> Let us develop the resources of our land, call forth its powers, build up its institutions, promote all its great interests, and see whether we also, in our day and generation, may not perform something worthy to be remembered.

Above this blue line, Gilbert crowned the chamber with spectators' galleries, symbolic figures, and the Capitol's largest murals. The galleries, fitted with steep banks of chairs upholstered in red, occupy the east and west arches. Circular medallions above each corner hold personifications of four virtues, painted by Arthur Willett from Garnsey's designs. Each depicts a strong seated woman, holding traditional symbols of Equality, Justice, Freedom, and Courage. But the real stars of the chamber, in size, scope, and fame, are Edwin Blashfield's murals. Like LaFarge, Blashfield was lionized as a leader of the mural movement in America. *The Minneapolis Journal* introduced him to readers as "the father of municipal art" in 1903: "Mr. Blashfield has varied talents. He is one of the ablest lecturers in the country, and he has employed his gifts in pressing art interests." Blashfield numbered the dome of the Library of Congress, courtrooms in New York and Baltimore, hotels, banks, and mansions among his mural commissions. His work often combined historical figures with imagined or symbolic ones, in frieze-like compositions that were well fitted to their architectural frames.

Blashfield drew on this signature style for two thirty-foot-wide allegories that offered his Minnesota viewers a mythology for their state. A contemporary critic who called these lunettes "beyond a doubt his finest works" summed up Blashfield's art:

> Each person reads into an allegory—if the title be lost sight of—his own temperament. Some one suggested that the two peasants in Millet's *Angelus* were not praying, but mourning over the rotten potatoes. But no one will ever say foolish things in the presence of these panels. They are too beautiful to provoke frivolity, too majestic to admit of vulgar associations, too entirely a part of the studied architecture of the imposing Senate chamber to be less than respected and too rich and harmonious in colour to allow any one to wish for the restoration of the virgin wall.

Visitors at the end of the twentieth century are unlikely to take these murals so seriously, after decades of iconoclastic art, but they can admire Blashfield's monumental essays in myth-making.

The north lunette, known by the unwieldy title *The Discoverers and Civilizers Led to the Source of the Mississippi,* presents his vision of Minnesota's great river. As in the Rotunda, Julie Gauthier's guidebook helps one decipher the artist's messages. Here Blashfield cast a white-robed Indian elder against somber pines as "the great Manitou, the chief god of the Indians." He holds an urn, from which the continent's longest river flows past an Indian couple, stock figures suggestive of Longfellow's *Song of Hiawatha* and Wild West shows. Other figures in the dress of the missionary, the courtly but well-armed explorer, and sundry pioneers approach the banks at the behest of two winged "Spirits of Civilization." Across the chamber hangs *Minnesota, the Granary of the World.* It, too, is built around a central figure—the white-robed lady Minnesota, drawn forward by a brace of snow-white oxen. This allegory of swords and plowshares contrasts Minnesotans of the Civil War with "men and women engaged in peaceful pursuits, over which the Spirit of Agriculture hovers, carrying corn and other grains." Blashfield inserted portraits of Gilbert and Seabury in modern dress at the Spirit's side, in a tribute that harkens back to the European practice of portraying the artist's patrons in an altarpiece commission.

Blashfield summoned up this cast of characters to give Minnesotans an imagery that might grace their state with a touch of the universal, while celebrating its uniqueness. His friend Kenyon Cox lamented the problems facing muralists in a commission like this:

> In asking that our public buildings be decorated with paintings related to our own history our people are only asking what every other people has asked since time immemorial. Unfortunately, our history is short, our costume is formless and ugly, and American historical subjects particularly unfitted for pictorial and, especially, decorative treatment.

Late twentieth century eyes look harshly on allegorical paintings like the Senate lunettes. But Blashfield considered his work "the art of embellishing the background of life." His murals, once set into place, were intended to provide a beautiful and thoughtful backdrop, not to claim the center of attention. Blashfield made a career of bridging the gap between the homely details of life and the glories of art. He devoted his great skills of drawing and composition with equal care to an army nurse and a harvest deity, to the wheel of a plow and an angel's wing.

Less deliberate juxtapositions are common throughout the Capitol: here in the Senate chamber, for example, the busts of Senators Nelson and Rice look a bit forlorn behind two photocopying machines. The action on the Senate floor has itself seemed at times like an ironic commentary on Blashfield's grand conceits. In 1937, for example, protestors of the radical People's Lobby stormed the Senate and occupied the chamber overnight. "The proceedings of the group were more informal than those of the usual occupants," observed the *St. Paul Pioneer Press:* "About 200 persons, including about 50 women, settled down to sleep in the Senate chamber shortly after midnight following a lunch of sandwiches, milk and beer." The *Minneapolis Tribune* reported that "they lounged in the senators' chairs, feet propped on the desks; those that couldn't find chairs sat on the floor. Others gathered around the rostrum singing songs and making speeches as the spirit moved them." The protestors left the next morning, leaving editors to fume over "the greatest disgrace in the history of the state."

The Senate chamber, like many other Capitol spaces, was remodeled in the 1970s. A new color scheme was overlaid on Gilbert and Garnsey's work, with their bold accents of blue and gold giving way to pink and red panels in the walls and dome. The huge wall sconces en-

Conservator James S. Horns cleaning Blashfield's mural
The Discoverers and Civilizers Led to the Source of the Mississippi, *1988.*

crusted with gilt-plaster ornament were removed, and a circular state
seal took the place of Garnsey's "Venetian pattern in gold" behind the
Senate leader's chair. This remodeling was thorough in its substitu-
tion of one period's palette for another. But in 1988 the Senate under-
took a total restoration project that returned the Chamber to its original splendor.

Legislators have their special chambers, corresponding to the Justices' Consultation Room. Studded leather doors flanking the Senate
rostrum open to the Senate Retiring Room. While the judges confer in
a room modeled on Independence Hall's courtroom, the senators step
into a room of self-consciously royal luxury. "It reminds one of some
of the rooms in the Palace of Versaille [sic] in its general arrangement
and furnishing," Gauthier wrote. "Long, French windows which are
partly covered by heavy red draperies embroidered with gold, open
upon a marble balcony, and a fireplace of red Numidian marble occupies either end of the room." This rich African marble is set within
wooden mantels carved with plant and animal motifs: bulls' heads at
the south end, goats' heads at the north.

The walls and ceilings boast equally ornate treatments, with deep

tones of crimson and painted patterns of oak and laurel—plants tra-
ditionally associated with dignity, strength, and honor. Garnsey described the effect of mellow age he sought: "The gilding and ground
color has been glazed down to the tone of a fine old book-binding, and
is in harmony with the old crimson and gold of the window hangings
and carpet." Furniture of mahogany and tufted leather completes the
Retiring Room's sumptuous appointments.

The visitor who finds the Senate chamber's atmosphere aristo-
cratic, and that of the Supreme Court elite, might look to the House
of Representatives for the common touch. Not so. Peering through
bronze gates into the House chamber, the only somber note to be
seen is the black suit Abe Lincoln wears in a portrait over the
Speaker's chair. The chamber is a feast of intricate floral decorations,
painted within fields of bright gold. It is Elmer Garnsey's showpiece,
the first major space to be completed while the other muralists
dabbed away in their Eastern studios. Garnsey's words best convey
the room's decor, from the top down:

> There is an elaborate skylight in the center of the ceiling, and from
> this a great coved surface descends to the gallery level. . . . A broad
> frieze encircles the skylight, the ground of which is gilded, and
> painted ornament is carried over the surface in ivory, green and red.
> The pendentives between the arches also have a gold ground, with
> elaborate designs of oak, laurel, cartouches, eagles, etc. . . . The wall
> panels are in gray red, with borders of dull yellow, and the capitals of
> the marble columns are gilded.

This lavish decor, like the prose in which Garnsey tallied its riches
for a 1905 *Western Architect* magazine article, may dazzle the visitor
at first. But this chamber, too, has its reigning geometry to anchor it
firmly within the larger scheme of the "grand floor." The House
chamber fills the north wing with its semicircular space, a broad
curving plan that is echoed in the alignment of the members' desks
and the arches overhead. The largest chamber in the Capitol, it seats
Minnesota's 134 representatives. Joint legislative sessions and special
events like the inaugurations of governors fill the chamber far beyond
the original space needed for the 1905 House of 119 members.

Gilbert's letters indicate that he first envisioned the House as a
modestly finished space. He wrote to Seabury in the spring of 1903,
"My idea in the House of Representatives is to keep the decorations
very simple and to rely upon the fine proportions of the room, using

House of Representatives Chamber, circa 1905. *The arch at right today holds the Brioschis' sculpture group* Minnesota – Spirit of Government.

only such colors as will tend to increase the appearance of size and to simplify the somewhat complex form of the room." In succeeding months he and Garnsey became an effective team, advancing the cause of harmonious decoration on both aesthetic and diplomatic fronts. Garnsey was often in St. Paul, where he served as advocate and spokesman for the art program to journalists and commissioners alike. Gilbert, for his part, fended off attacks on the chief decorator from envious local artists and from unions objecting to Garnsey's employment of New York painters to decorate Minnesota's statehouse. Garnsey's proposal for the House clearly pleased the commissioners, who ultimately paid Garnsey $125,500 for decorations throughout the statehouse, instead of the $50,000 of his original contract.

Garnsey tailored his work to Minnesota by including native wildflowers in the decorative designs, and by lettering the names of the region's French explorers on the ceiling. And as in other second floor spaces, he let the voices of the past speak from the House walls by let-

tering lengthy quotations on the great arch above the Speaker's desk:
Jefferson's proclamation of the rights to "life, liberty, and the pursuit
of happiness" from the Declaration of Independence, paired with
Patrick Henry's exhortation in favor of "a frequent recurrence to fun-
damental principles."

This is one of the rare spaces that has been enriched, rather than
injured, by remodeling. The arch above the Speaker of the House
originally held a spectators' gallery, but the House needed more
space. Walled off from public view and divided into two floors in 1938,
the gallery provided new offices and committee rooms. Funds from
the State Emergency Relief Act made it possible to commission a
sculpture group by a father-and-son team. Carlo Brioschi, an Italian
immigrant to St. Paul, and his son Amerigo reinterpreted the Capitol's turn-of-the-century symbols and types with a classic 'Thirties solidity. Made of painted plaster before a patterned, gilded wall, *Minnesota—Spirit of Government* stands as a haloed goddess on a
pedestal that bears the state seal. To her right one sees an Indian man
and woman; to her left, a trapper and voyageur. A ringing non-
sequitur below proclaims "The Trail of the Pioneer Bore the Foot-
prints of Liberty." Obscured beneath the handiwork of the 1930s re-
modelers, ironically, were the allegorical figures of *History* and
Records, painted by W. A. Mackay from Garnsey's designs.

For the House Retiring Room, Gilbert and Garnsey added Minnesota motifs to a room that follows European models. Gauthier described the "delightfully agreeable effect":

> It is like a room in some old Italian or French chateau of the time of
> Francis the First. The idea was suggested by Mr. Gilbert who made
> studies for it in pencil, which were elaborated and perfected in color
> by Mr. Garnsey. Above a high wainscot of a dark, dull-colored oak, is a
> frieze resembling tapestry, which suggests a dense forest in a misty,
> grey light with occasional glints of sunshine, and a mass of flowers
> near the lower edge. Although treated conventionally the trees and
> flowers can readily be recognized as characteristic of Minnesota.

The painted wildflowers and trees, casual compared to the House
chamber's symmetrical ornaments, add gentle touches of color to the
dark paneled room.

When the House of Representatives restored its chamber in 1989,
the guiding spirit of fidelity to Gilbert and Garnsey's original designs
met the realities of the room's long working life. Many decisions were

House of Representatives Retiring Room, circa 1907.

simple. The portrait of Abraham Lincoln remained over the Speaker's chair. A copy of G. P. A. Healy's 1887 painting by St. Paul's Edward V. Brewer, the portrait was not part of the chamber's original plan. But custom and sentiment dictated that it be returned to its place of honor at the end of the restoration process. The House added another portrait at the time: a bronze bust by Paul Granlund of Chief Clerk Edward A. Burdick was placed in the vestibule of the chamber he had overseen since 1967.

An exhaustive study of all painted surfaces guided the repainting of walls in their original colors, while the cleaning of Garnsey's decorations removed decades of accumulated smoke and dirt. Formica paneling that covered the members' desks was an "improvement" that was discarded in good conscience, so that the mahogany desks, fitted with new microphones and other electronic gear, could be restored to their original appearance. In the process, however, traces of their time-honored uses (including the carved initials of some past representatives) were obliterated in the interest of prettier surfaces. The Brioschis' sculptures were retained as artworks that had earned their own place in the history of a statehouse that has adapted to the people's needs and whims for nearly a century.

Figurehead and Front Lawn

$\mathcal{T}$HE SAME CURIOSITY that leads visitors through the Capitol's long halls often makes them want to get behind the scenes. Capitol tours offer an occasional glimpse of the bones and structure inside the building. Better still, the visitor can climb to the roof for a close-up look at the Quadriga, and a panoramic view of the Capitol area and the city spreading out around it. No elegant decorations line this stage of one's Capitol exploration. Instead, the visitor goes behind a locked third-floor door and mounts a curving steel stairway. Bare lightbulbs and the echoes of footfalls add to the eerie passage. But soon the visitor emerges into fresh air and strong breezes at the base of the dome.

The view takes many visitors by surprise. Perhaps expecting to see gilded statues or downtown skyscrapers, they arrive at rooftop level on the dome's north side, looking over the skylight of the House chamber. A brick walkway leads around to the Quadriga, but few visitors care to rush. Most pause to take in the view along University Avenue, looking west past the houses and churches of the Frogtown and Midway neighborhoods to the skyline of Minneapolis on the horizon. Those who walk around the eastward side of the dome see a complex of hospital buildings, the swooping interchanges of two major freeways, and the Mississippi River in the distance. The river passes between Dayton's Bluff on the city's East Side, and the runways of Holman Field, a commuter airport opposite. The Mississippi here is neither the wooded stream Edwin Blashfield imagined in his Senate Chamber mural, nor the miles-wide Big Muddy of St. Louis or New Orleans. But it is a working river in St. Paul. From the Capitol roof one can see fleets of barges loaded with grain and coal.

From this rooftop vantage one realizes just how big the Capitol is. The roof covers nearly two acres. Skylights above the stair halls and major chambers mark the paths and places the visitor has experienced inside. These utilitarian features have a visual interest of their own, in the mix of materials, colors, and decorative touches. Copper

View from the Capitol roof to downtown St. Paul, circa *1925.*

roof panels and moldings, turned a soft green from decades' exposure to the weather, contrast with the white marble dome. Curving brackets and small decorative crests on the copper ridges recall the motifs seen on furniture inside; the ridge along the House skylight is studded with animal heads. Flagpoles rise like plant stalks from leaf-shaped copper bosses at the center of the Senate, House, and Court chamber skylights.

The roof has had leaks since its first construction, a fact that will not surprise anyone who considers the challenge of such a large, complex flat roof in a severe northern climate. Garnsey wrote to Gilbert in 1904, "My foreman at the Minnesota State Capitol reports as follows: 'The East and West Dome Corridors have leaks which will ruin our decorations. These have existed a long time, and should be repaired at once, so we may proceed with the work.'" Decades later, legislators occasionally had to step around buckets beneath leaking skylights in their chambers. Some simply sat under umbrellas at their desks, to stay dry and to point out the need for an immediate repair. A complete re-roofing job is scheduled to be done before the year

2000. As in the interior restorations of the 1980s, this will afford an opportunity to preserve the original appearance and materials, and keep the Capitol's occupants dry in its second century.

East or west, the walk around the dome leads one to the Quadriga. Placed like a figurehead at the crest of the Capitol, its massive horses and earnest figures so dazzle visitors that they forget mundane concerns like leaky roofs. Here one stands side-by-side with the vision of progress that the Capitol's builders held. From the sidewalks below, the Quadriga appeared as a distant ornament. Up close, one is impressed not just by its glittering surfaces but by the size and power of its sculpted forms. Standing high on a Minnesota rooftop with four golden horses and a trio of figures in flowing draperies can help even a jaded visitor, if only for a moment, share the turn-of-the-century taste for pomp and splendor.

Gilbert's desire to grace the Capitol with sculpture is evident in his earliest sketches. His competition drawing of 1895 shows not just a quadriga group, but freestanding figures flanking it at the corners of the central bay. The realization of the Quadriga, like the artful decorations inside, had to await the legislature's approval of more funds than originally planned. But Gilbert was already exploring the idea of a classically inspired triumphal monument with Daniel Chester French. The architect tempered his hopes with inquiries about the relative costs of casting the Quadriga in bronze, the preferred material for durability and subtleties of surface and touch, or the less costly option of sheet copper, formed over a metal framework. Regardless of the choice of metals, Gilbert planned to gild the surfaces, "to emphasize this focal point in the design by a spot of brilliant light," as he later explained to a St. Paul newspaper. In 1903 French signed a contract to execute the sculpture group in copper, but not without a complaint about the $35,000 budget allowed for the Quadriga. He wrote to Gilbert, "You can tell Mr. Seabury that prices of the sculptors have about doubled in the last six or eight years, so that really he is getting a great deal for his money." French also groused about the workload which his success as one of America's preeminent sculptors had brought. "As to time, how do you suppose I am going to make the Custom House groups, the St. Louis statuary, and all the other things you are looking to me for in my lifetime?" he wrote, in reference to his work on Gilbert's New York Custom House and 1904 Louisiana Purchase Exposition projects. "I do not see how I can do anything

Workmen sanding the Quadriga for a 1949 re-gilding.

about the Quadriga for a year at least, and I think we shall have to set three years as the limit of time in the contract."

For all his grumbling, French set to work on the Capitol commission immediately. His letters indicate how French adapted his earlier quadriga from the World's Columbian Exposition to Minnesota:

> You will be glad to know that I have begun a model for the central figure (in the chariot) of the Quadriga. The other figures are already designed, as are the horses, since we are to follow the Quadriga which presided over the Columbian Arch at Chicago . . . The central figure, representing Columbus would, of course, not be appropriate for the State Capitol of Minnesota, so that a new design for this figure is necessary.

French's letter further illustrates how casually the artists of the American Renaissance movement could assign a meaning to a statue, and vice versa. "As the two figures leading the horses are female figures, I think the figure in the chariot should be a male figure," he wrote. "I think it should represent 'Minnesota', if you think that a male figure can personify a state." French placed in his charioteer's hand a tall staff on which hangs a banner with the legend "MINNESOTA."

Despite French's concern for the symbolism of his figures, most visitors respond to and remember Potter's golden horses. Ask a class of fourth graders about their Capitol tour, and most will eagerly describe the horses on the roof. Look up newspaper articles on the Quadriga's history: headlines identify it as the "golden horse sculpture." The broad, muscular beasts capture a visitor's attention for their earthy strength. They do their job of symbolizing the forces of Nature well. The two female figures, holding the bridles as symbols of Woman's controlling and directing influence, may be "full of life, strength and grace," as Gauthier judged. But the animals add a bold, energetic note to a building whose business is order and restraint.

French sculpted the charioteer model at his studio in western Massachusetts. Edward Potter joined him there to transform their Columbus quadriga into a fit emblem for Minnesota's statehouse. French persisted in his hopes of casting the group in bronze, offering to do so for an additional $5,000 as late as spring 1906. But Gilbert conveyed the Board's refusal: "However much they would like to use bronze they have not the money available for this purpose, as their appropriation is now all engaged in finishing up various minor items which are regarded as essential." French accordingly had the Quadriga executed in sheet copper, whose carefully soldered seams can be seen by observant visitors.

The sculptures were installed on the Capitol roof later in 1906. Metal rods were soon attached to the male figure to brace it against the wind. The following spring, the St. Paul firm of Bazille & Partridge gilded the sculptures according to Gilbert's instructions. The architect had told French how he "stated to the Board that in my opinion this sculpture should not be given a brilliant gilding, but that it should be a dull gold." The initial effect when the gilders completed their work was nonetheless startling. Seabury, in a rare aesthetic dispute with the architect, found the Quadriga's brilliance out of harmony with the building, and urged that it be toned down.

Dazzling in full sunlight or muted by overcast skies, the gilded finish of the Quadriga makes it one of the Capitol's most prominent fea-

tures. It has long been a staple image of postcards and tourism
brochures. It regularly hovers behind television journalists during
their coverage of news from the statehouse. But it has had its critics,
and few have been more vocal than the Minnesota pioneer turned
cowboy poet Hanford Lennox Gordon. Known as "Thundering Gordon," he had practiced law at St. Cloud, worked in the lumber business in Minneapolis, and enlisted in the army in the Civil War. Gordon's writings celebrated the First Minnesota's charge at Gettysburg,
and recast Indian legends in verse. Moving to California in 1892, he
published *Cowboy Ballads* and other volumes. But on a visit to Minnesota in 1910 he turned his pen against the Quadriga and its classical references in lively published letters about "Them Gilded Bronchos (sic):"

> A few days ago I went down to St. Paul to see the new capitol, your
> grand all around new capitol, and my heart fell 40 degrees and over
> when I saw a lot of "gilded bricks," Roman bricks, on top of your (oth-
> erwise) splendid capitol. I don't know who did it, and I don't care to
> criticize men. But, look here, they (those Roman horses and the char-
> iot) don't represent Minnesota, not one corner of it from Winona to
> Pembina.

Gordon called for direct action: "Take a sledge hammer and smash
'them' Roman bronchos and that chariot! Clean 'em out and put a
grand heroic statue of Alexander Ramsey in their stead . . . ." His dia-
tribe sparked letters and editorials, for and against the Quadriga, the
Capitol's architecture and expense, and the practice of clothing public buildings in classical allegories.

Thundering Gordon warmed to his theme in other letters, ex-
pounding on the glories of Minnesota's past with especially purple
prose reserved for "Bluff Old Aleck" Ramsey. A writer identified only
as "Justice" countered with an ironic suggestion:

> The figures on the Capitol represent the return of a victorious gen-
> eral, which at that time represented 'modern progress'; if he [Gordon]
> wants something to represent that manly and heroic man, why not
> have a group cast with 'Bluff Old Aleck' killing an Indian, to represent
> the 'modern progress' of us Anglo-Saxons?

The press in other communities joined the dialogue. Duluth's *News-
Tribune* turned its editorial on the "brazen nags" into an attack on
Gilbert:

The trouble with the gentleman, when he designed the capitol, was that he forgot this was Minnesota in North America and not Italy. The whole marble excrescence has no proper place in this land of hard, brilliant sunlight and winter snows and its brass colored horses are no more of an unnatural effrontery than is the rest.

Others supported Gilbert and the Quadriga. The *Pioneer Press* predicted that "those who admire the structure can keep on admiring. And those who do not admire will without doubt keep on not admiring. And there will be diversity of opinion to the end of time, or rather, till time shall create here a ruin beyond criticism."

The Quadriga weathered the tirades of 1910. Since that time it has needed periodic regilding and repairs to weather Minnesota's climate. Its placement on the façade exposes the sculpture to ninety-degree summers, subzero winters, and strong winds year 'round. The Quadriga is also vulnerable to the attentions of its admirers. Generations of tourists and pranksters have rubbed the gilded surfaces, frolicked on the horses, and carved their initials into the sculptures. Each generation of custodians has done its best to maintain the Quadriga, repairing and regilding it in 1949 and again in 1979. A novel, high-profile event, the gilding of the horses has attracted news coverage each time. But the questioning of the Quadriga's meaning has softened to affection and pride. Artist LeRoy Neiman, who grew up nearby in the Frogtown neighborhood, made the horses of the Quadriga the subject of his Bicentennial painting *The Baghdad of the Midwest*, now in the collection of the Minnesota Museum of American Art.

The damage, vandalism, wear and tear of eight decades prompted thorough examinations of the Quadriga in the 1990s. Art conservators brought a battery of resources from the fields of art, science, and history. The professional conservator's emphasis on first preserving as much original material as possible, and then restoring missing or damaged features, has a kinship with the conservation of natural resources. Both disciplines have a concern for underlying causes, as well as easily visible features. A biologist will study the water quality, plant life, and human influence on a habitat, where a layperson might see only the bright plumage of ducks on the pond. Similarly, conservators of artworks test the health of the often hidden structures that support the gilded finish.

A 1993 examination of abrasions on the Quadriga's gilding

(caused by the rubbing of tarpaulins meant to protect the sculptures during roof repairs) showed other signs of damage. Tiny pockmarks indicated corrosion beneath the gilding. Split seams showed where wind and weather had fractured the copper. Water penetrating through these cracks further weakened the internal structures of each sculpture, including the chariot. A reexamination the following spring showed that conditions were quickly worsening. Fearing that the strain of one more winter might finally knock the "gilded bron- chos" off the Capitol, officials brought specialists in sculpture conser- vation to St. Paul. Working with an engineer to analyze the sculp- tures' condition and with historians to search out evidence of just how the sculptors and architect wanted the sculptures to look, con- servators removed the Quadriga from the Capitol in the summer of 1994 for a thorough restoration of its structure and surfaces. Done in conjunction with the re-roofing of the building, the Quadriga restora- tion will enable visitors to see the sculptures much as they first ap- peared. They can keep on admiring or keep on not admiring, as St. Paul's editors foresaw, well into the twenty-first century.

A visitor on the rooftop can look across manicured grounds, some- times called "Minnesota's front lawn," to see how history has fulfilled French's notion of *The Progress of the State*. The growth of Min- nesota's population is visible not just in St. Paul's downtown sky- scrapers and high-rise apartments, but in water towers on the hori- zon that mark the spread of suburban towns. Freeways link the Capitol to communities across the state. The visitor can also see at closer range the growth of government, embodied in a district of state buildings and monuments erected since the Quadriga first crowned the Capitol.

A concern for the proper setting of Minnesota's statehouse was im- plied in its earliest documents. The 1894 "Act to Provide for a New Capitol" specified that the statehouse be built "upon a lot surrounded by streets or open ground." An orator at the 1898 cornerstone cere- mony spoke of "a domed building, with impressive approaches" as the ideal form for a capitol, suggesting a fit between building and set- ting that should be more than just practical. Like the architecture and decorations of the building, Gilbert's plans for the Capitol grounds deliberately evoke precedents in European cities, in Wash- ington, D. C., and in the seminal example of the World's Columbian Exposition of 1893. His plans for St. Paul featured broad avenues that focus long views on key buildings and monuments, radiating street plans, and classical structures that affect a genteel Old World air.

If the Capitol building embodies Gilbert's spirit, the history of the Capitol area evokes his ghost, hovering unseen but strongly felt by later architects, urban planners, and landscape designers. Gilbert defined a vision of the Capitol as the focal point of a system of broad avenues laid in elegant symmetry across St. Paul. In subsequent decades, planners initiated, modified, thwarted, and resurrected Capitol area plans which were touted as the heirs to his vision. The visitor can look over the cumulative result of these activities. Where Gilbert imagined an ideal city plan, the visitor can see reality: a complex of buildings, streets, monuments and vistas shaped as much by urban dynamics, politics, finances, and especially the automobile as by any master plan. A broad sidewalk leads from the Capitol steps, in line with Gilbert's intended primary axis for the area. Cedar Street and John Ireland Boulevard fan out from the statehouse, with a pair of government buildings fronting each to acknowledge the symmetry he demanded. But state buildings of the 1950s diverge in style from Gilbert's classicism; the view down the main axis is closed by a fifth building, the Veterans Service Building; and a belt of highways separates the Capitol from the city that Gilbert's plan was to unite.

This viewpoint alongside the Quadriga offers little evidence of the houses, shops, churches, and schools that once made up a neighborhood. Some houses were bought and cleared as early as the 1890s to make room for the Capitol building. Others, including late nineteenth century mansions on the height of ground behind the Capitol, survived into the 1960s. Central Park, a congenial Victorian amenity nearby, disappeared into the Capitol area's gravitational pull. A bakery contributed its heady aroma to the area, until it too was razed in 1993. But the statehouse began to change this part of the city while it was still on the drawing boards. The Board of State Capitol Commissioners had authority to acquire land, and Seabury drove his usual hard bargains to enlarge the grounds while the Capitol was under construction.

Gilbert was planning the Capitol's surroundings, even as he was devoting personal attention to endless details of its interior construction and finish. No detail, inside or out, seemed too small for his concern. His papers include drawings of trees and shrubs, sketched in heavy black ink to illustrate his goals: "In planting as in arranging a

STATE CAPITOL AND CENTRAL PARK. ST. PAUL. MINN.

Central Park, the Capitol, and neighboring houses
shown in a postcard, circa 1915.

bouquet of flowers some experiment must be tried. The whole planting is a matter of design not whim and must relate to the architecture
as a whole or it will be worse than useless and a waste of money."
Memoranda preserve the evolution of his larger plans. "It is expected
that in provision for suitable approaches the City of St. Paul, appreci-
ating the advantages of the location of the Capitol in this City, will
provide handsome and suitable approaches by re-arranging streets,
forming broad avenues bordered by appropriate and handsome municipal, art, and historic buildings," said a 1904 press release about
the nearly complete statehouse. Gilbert also sought support through
presentations to civic groups. An officer of St. Paul's Women's Civic
League pledged her group's help after the architect addressed the
League on the Capitol's potential as the catalyst for a grand city plan.
"The views of what other cities have make us long for the time when
the possibilities you showed us should become facts," she wrote in
reference to Gilbert's slides of streets and gardens in France, Italy,
and Massachusetts.

By the end of 1904, Gilbert could outline his vision in a seven page
memorandum. He proposed enlarging the Capitol grounds by relocat-
ing a school building "of inferior construction and very bad design,"
removing streetcar tracks, and creating a larger, more symmetrical

General view from Gilbert's Capitol Approach Plan,
published in 1907.

immediate setting than the Capitol then enjoyed. Three main "lines
of approach" would link the Capitol to the business district along
Cedar Street, to the "best resident district" along Summit Avenue,
and straight south from the Capitol façade to Seven Corners, an intersection on the western edge of downtown St. Paul. A park halfway
to Seven Corners would be the site of a Soldiers Monument; public
gardens would grace the three lines of approach. Gilbert estimated
the cost of his plan at two million dollars.

The history of Gilbert's dream of making his Capitol the catalyst
for a splendid urban design is one of frustrations and paper plans.
"Like many of America's grand Beaux Arts schemes, the Gilbert plan
was never fully realized," wrote architectural historians David Gebhard and Tom Martinson, "but one can obtain some idea of its
breadth and scale by wandering around the grounds to the south of
the Capitol and by viewing the building from various points on the
east bank of the river." Gilbert's early efforts earned him a prominent
role in St. Paul planning commissions. He also found some allies in
the legislature. Representative James Hickey, for one, wrote to the *St.
Paul Globe*, "I think that the grounds adjacent to the State Capitol
should be in keeping with the magnificent building itself . . . In but
few states in America can be seen such a building as the great marble

palace on the hill." The editors agreed: "No such building as this can produce its proper effect if it is cramped in diminutive grounds or surrounded by dwarfed or unsightly buildings. The eye must travel over generous spaces that fit in with the generous proportions of the capitol itself in order to comprehend it as a whole." Gilbert prepared an ambitious 1907 document illustrating the boulevards and buildings that St. Paul could create in future years, but civic momentum and funding failed to match his dreams. More effective initiatives came from the construction of state buildings in later decades. Between 1915 and 1917 the Minnesota Historical Society erected a building on Cedar Street to house collections that had outgrown its rooms in the basement of the Capitol. The columned façade of Clarence H. Johnston, Sr.'s design echoes the Capitol's classicism in warm-toned Minnesota granite.

The need for state office space in the 1920s reopened debate over Capitol area development. Members of a state building commission divided in their preferences for a building site north of the Capitol on University Avenue, or one flanking the statehouse on Wabasha Street. Gilbert was engaged to reassess his 1907 Capitol approach plan with an eye toward defining future building locations. His 1931 "restudy" confirmed and expanded the original scheme. Following Gilbert's strong recommendation, the State Office Building was built to Johnston's design on the Wabasha Street site in 1932. Here it provided a symmetrical partner to the Historical Society Building across the lawns. Its size, style, and material reinforce its kinship to Johnston's earlier building for the Historical Society, and the two granite structures team with the Capitol to establish the area's fan-shaped orientation.

The Capitol area that a visitor sees from the statehouse roof took its definitive shape after World War II. Plans for postwar highway construction, a war memorial, and a state building to serve the needs of returning veterans all intersected in the Capitol area. Architect Johnston worked with landscape specialists Arthur R. Nichols and George Nason of Morell and Nichols Inc. to create a state government complex, bounded by a highway to be built between the Capitol and St. Paul's downtown business district. Their plan paid tribute to Gilbert's Beaux-Arts concepts, but recognized that the automobile was a powerful force in mid-twentieth century America. Nichols, like Gilbert before him, noted the need for open space. "People need space. It

Aerial view of the Capitol neighborhood in the winter of 1928-1929.

means freedom and beauty," he told an interviewer in 1970. The postwar plan provided ample lawns, a site directly south of the Capitol for a Veterans Service Building, and a Court of Honor to consist of a rose garden and memorial plaques. Architect W. Brooks Cavin, Jr. won the national competition for the veterans building in 1946 with a design that exemplified "modern architecture" to Minnesotans. The granite building of interlocking shapes struck citizens as simultaneously severe and elegant, with its central mass spanning an open space that allows one to look from the Capitol steps straight through to downtown.

As World War II ended, the southern edge of the Capitol area was still home to several thousand St. Paulites who resisted the state's first calls to move. The rundown properties were a recent memory when Carol Brink wrote *The Twin Cities*, published in 1961: "The approach to the capitol used to be cluttered with tenements and rickety buildings of all sorts. Once for a couple of years I conducted a girls' club in the basement of one of the old churches, and for the first time I became aware that we had slums in St. Paul, and that they were only

Demolition of apartment buildings to enlarge the Capitol area, 1956.

a stone's throw from the State Capitol building . . . " Relocation of these residents and clearance of the land was a slow process. Cavin's Veterans Service Building was not ready for occupancy until 1953–54, and its construction not fully completed until 1973.

By the late 1950s, the expansion of state government once more created an acute need for office space. The Transportation Building (originally called the Highway Building) was built along John Ireland Boulevard in 1956–58; the Centennial Building (named in honor of the hundredth anniversary of statehood) was erected along Cedar Street in 1958–60. Both extended the fan-shaped alignment begun by Johnston's Historical Society and State Office Buildings; both used granite, glass, and steel to clothe their boxy, flat façades. Ellerbe Architects' design for the Transportation Building called originally for a six-story office structure. Last-minute lobbying in the 1957 legislative session authorized its expansion to eight stories, a height that made the building's "Corporate International" style far too prominent for many critics. The Centennial Building by Thorshov and Cerny struck many observers as even more anonymous. With a façade like an IBM punch card, it epitomized 'Fifties conformity all too well.

With a campus of state buildings and open spaces established by 1960, Minnesotans began to look for ways to steer their Capitol area through the complex issues of city planning and urban renewal. Many were dissatisfied with the inferior designs of the Transportation and Centennial Buildings, and also wanted to enhance the grounds of their statehouse. In 1967 the Capitol Area Architectural and Planning Commission was formed, to preserve the Capitol building, prepare plans for the Capitol area, and conduct competitions for new buildings in the area. This commission, later renamed a Board, erected no building of its own. Yet its activities since 1967 have influenced all aspects of the Capitol area that one sees today.

Beginning in 1968 with a widely publicized effort to halt construction of a gas station near the Capitol, the CAAPB embraced the concept of Gilbert's Capitol as the center of a district extending in all directions. CAAPB plans of the 1970s and 80s refined that concept into landscape and use zones that have distinctive characters of their own. Each comprehensive plan has reflected the thinking of its time about commercial development and tourist amenities, parks and parking lots. A proposal for a Capitol Building Annex led the CAAPB to hold a "National Terratectural Competition" in 1976–77 for a legislative and museum complex to be built *under* the Capitol lawn. The winning design, by Helmut Jahn of Chicago's C. F. Murphy Associates, featured skylit underground gardens as well as hearing rooms and a history museum. This imaginative design response to maintaining an unobstructed view of the Capitol façade never left the drawing board. As with other grand plans in the Capitol area, a lack of consensus and funding kept the project unbuilt.

As appreciation of the Capitol's architecture and decoration deepened in the 1980s, Capitol area plans extended a postmodern classicism to the neighborhood of the statehouse. The spirit of Gilbert's original ideas was honored by the closing of several streets, to strengthen the area's symmetry while easing the automobile's grip on the complex. New space needs were addressed by preserving the façades of earlier buildings, while enlarging their interiors. The State Office Building was renovated in 1986, with an additional floor added behind its 1932 façade. Across the Capitol lawn, Minnesota's court system found a home within the former Historical Society Building. Designed by Leonard Parker and Associates, the Minnesota Judicial Center occupies a full block behind Johnston's original building. The Minnesota History Center, completed in 1992 to the designs of Hammel, Green, and Abrahamson, stretches the boundaries of the Capitol area beyond the freeways. Built of native stone and oriented to views of the Capitol and Cathedral, the History Center rivals the statehouse in size and materials.

The view from the Capitol rooftop evolves by design, as successive generations interpret Cass Gilbert's ideas for a beautiful and logical urban order. A 1986 CAAPB competition invited designs for an urban landscape plan: not just Capitol approaches, but gathering spaces for year-round use. Proposals came in from as far away as Australia. The 180 designs ranged from classical symmetry to back-to-nature informality. Entrants proposed that the Capitol mall be planted with prairie grasses, paved with a miniature replica of Gilbert's early street plans, or fitted with ponds and skating rinks. But the competition judges' preference for classical design, in line with 1980s appreciation of architectural traditions, was clear in juror Leon Krier's statement: "I prefer a second-rate classical scheme to a first-rate modernist scheme." The winning design by David R. Mayernik and Thomas N. Rajkovich, working in association with Hammel, Green and Abrahamson, supplied a proudly neoclassical design that was nationally honored as first-rate.

The winning design featured a broad public square fronting the Capitol, to serve as a forum or gathering ground for political rallies and cultural events. A proposed "cascade" of water, "a lively, forceful display of nature," would lead to a reflecting pool flanked by lawns and trees. Terraces, richly ornamented with classical details, would line the Cedar Street approach to the Capitol. Mayernik and Rajkovich titled their proposal "Project for the Completion of the Capitol Mall," in recognition of their allegiance to Gilbert's classical design: "Our goal first and foremost was to complete Cass Gilbert's vision for the mall," Rajkovich stated. His partner articulated a design philosophy that echoed Gilbert and other turn-of-the-century apologists like Kenyon Cox. "Architecture is a kind of language," Mayernik told a New York Times reporter. "Modernism tries to reinvent language, but classicism simply tries to use the language that has existed for thousands of years."

Mayernik and Rajkovich successfully advocated a purist's classicism, even insisting on traditional masonry walls rather than less costly concrete construction techniques. The classicizing tendency of the 1980s also enhanced a series of bridges around the Capitol complex. State highway designers reconsidered freeway overpasses, which were due for rebuilding, as symbolic entries to the Capitol area. They added simulated stonework and old-fashioned lampposts, to mimic the Capitol's traditional details. While such decorations can be pleasing touches when seen from a moving car, they are likely to disappoint the visitor who leaves the Capitol to stroll the area. Freeway classicism, fabricated from precast concrete and hastily assembled steel railings, is best seen from a distance at highway speeds.

But larger plans for the Capitol area aim to guide its future development as an orderly evolution of Gilbert's ideas. The Mayernik-Rajkovich concept plan, which would cost nearly fifteen million dollars to build all at once, serves as a guide to the addition of memorials and other enhancements of the Capitol mall. The CAAPB master plans treat the Capitol area as a complex of housing, business, and office uses, a living neighborhood rather than just a setting for the statehouse. Through decades of fitful efforts, Minnesotans have evolved a working application of the ideal Gilbert foresaw:

> If one builds for the future, they may build extravagantly and unwisely, but if they plan for the future and build only that which is necessary or desirable at the present time, they will provide for posterity and add not only to their own pleasure, but to the value of their property and of the community in which they live.

History Lessons in Paint

*T*HE CAPITOL is full of discoveries waiting to be made, small pleasures which contrast with its grand features. The news that one granite column weighs more than nine tons may make visitors shake their heads in wonder; but the discovery of a little gopher carved on a picture frame makes them smile. The walk downstairs from the rooftop is a good opportunity to scout out these modest attractions, on the way to the Governor's Reception Room.

The halls become familiar territory to a visitor who has seen the sights in, around, and from the top of the Capitol. A glimpse of the Rotunda through columns, the sight of a mural, or perhaps just a water fountain one had noticed on the way up to the roof: these become landmarks on the mental map of the visitor. With this familiarity comes an enjoyment of features that may have been lost in the larger picture at first viewing. The visitor may notice now that the seven-foot-tall bronze lamp posts in the halls have eagles and classical figures cast in their bases. One may overhear other visitors sharing their discoveries: "Look at the ears of corn stenciled on the arches!" Gilbert sought artful solutions to basic functions. A public stairway to connect all the floors, for instance, offered the architect a chance to design a graceful winding stair in the northeast angle of the building. Cantilevered from the wall, the staircase needs minimal space to serve its purpose. But it also offers a graceful descent down marble steps worn smooth at the edges by ninety years' use. The main stair halls impel one to "mount, with two pauses for breath, straight to the second floor," an early visitor found. But the spiral stair invites the visitor to glide down a wide oval path, with a sculpted marble handrail set in the wall for a guide.

The spiral stair brings one to the first floor, face to face with Minnesota's governors. Portraits of the earlier governors hang in chronological order in the first floor halls; the sequence continues on the ground floor with more recent chief executives. This procession of oil paintings has an air of tradition, but the custom is only half as old as

Cantilevered staircase at the northeast corner of the Rotunda.

the Capitol. Gilbert had accommodated portraits of Minnesota's early governors on the walls of the governor's private office. In 1944, Governor Edward J. Thye ordered the additional portraits hung in the corridors "so that visitors entering the Capitol will have an opportunity to view them." State workers moved lamp posts from their original places by the red painted panels in the halls, to make room for the portraits. Keen-eyed visitors may notice marks on the floor showing where the lamp posts once stood, and find them in the new locations a few feet away.

As an artistic specialty, a governor's portrait offers limited scope for the painter's skills. The first portraits are bust-length likenesses with the frontier plainness of Minnesota's early years. Later nineteenth century governors were portrayed on a larger scale, some leaning on law books like image-conscious Victorian barristers. Governors of the twentieth century have at times stepped out of doors for portraits, and added personal touches that cue the viewer to their moment in Minnesota history. Floyd B. Olson, a media-wise politician who was drawing national attention before his untimely death in 1936, strikes a charismatic pose in the official portrait by Carl Bohnen. Cutting a natty figure in his gray double-breasted suit, Olson grasps a microphone as his symbol of authority. Other portraits hold more subtle hints of a sitter's official status. Nicholas R. Brewer, a prominent St. Paul artist who also restored LaFarge's Supreme Court murals in 1933, painted Governors John A. Johnson and Winfield S. Hammond in their Capitol armchairs. The unique gilded frame of Johnson's portrait is carved with the state's North Star, lady's-slipper, and gopher motifs.

A stroll to the first floor's west end brings the visitor to the suite of the governor. Gilbert designed suitably impressive rooms for Minnesota's highest official. "Mr. Gilbert remembered Venice when he designed the Governor's Reception Room, with its high oak wainscot and elaborately carved wood-work," Elmer Garnsey wrote. His fellow artist Kenyon Cox said the room was "conceived on the lines of a Venetian council chamber, with heavy, gilded moldings intended to frame historical pictures rather than decorations." Gilbert had begun with far more modest plans for the governor's suite. "The executive rooms should be finished in perfectly plain color without elaborate decoration of any kind," he told the Board in the same letter of May 1903 that carried his recommendations for murals elsewhere in the

Governor Floyd B. Olson *by Carl E. Bohnen,*
one of a series of governor's portraits in the Capitol halls.

Governor's Reception Room, circa *1970.*
Millet's Treaty of Traverse des Sioux *hangs in the background.*

Capitol. The evolution of the governor's suite was partly a response to Minnesotans' suggestions for pictures from their own history. But Gilbert, ever alert to opportunity and recharged by a European vacation of his own, transformed his conception of the rooms from executive simplicity to spaces which Julie Gauthier called "the most ornate in the building."

The combination of "Venetian" decor and history paintings creates an atmosphere unlike any other Capitol space. One enters the suite through an antechamber, and steps into the center of the Governor's Reception Room. It is a ceremonial room, designed for the rituals of state receptions, proclamations, and press conferences. It can serve as a meeting room or command center for the work of the governor's staff, especially during the intense months of activity when the legislature is in session. But to most Capitol visitors, the Governor's Reception Room is a hushed, elaborate, even excessive chamber. Each panel and molding is garnished with deeply carved shapes that are gilded, like the entire ceiling, in a mellow finish admired in Gilbert's day as "old gold." A close inspection reveals carved pine cones and ears of corn, cherubs and lions, Roman helmets and grotesque faces. Crystal chandeliers, light bulbs strung like pearls along the cornices, and a mantel of imported marbles add brighter touches to the heavily draped and upholstered setting. Gauthier spared no praise in describing its furnishings: "Gold-embroidered red window and door hangings, a red rug, light golden yellow leather chairs and sofas, and highly polished, natural colored mahogany tables and desks complete the finest room of its kind in the country."

One month after Gilbert described his plans for a very simple decor, General James H. Baker, Civil War veteran and officer of the Minnesota Historical Society, presented another viewpoint to the Capitol commissioners. He communicated the Society's wish for *Minnesota* subjects:

> I think that I fairly voice the sentiment of the people of our state when I say that we want no Greek or Roman antiques, however classic, no dancing nymphs or goddesses on the walls of the Capitol. The desire is to have our own local history illustrated, our own battles, our own heroes, our own barbarians, our own lakes and rivers.

Baker enumerated topics like "a herd of buffaloes, now almost extinct, but once the lords of our prairies" and the voyageurs of the fur trade, "those pioneers of the commerce of Lake Superior, gliding along the blue bosom of the great lakes in the twilight of our history."

But the Historical Society's first choice for a Minnesota history painting was the signing of the Treaty of Traverse des Sioux. This meeting of Dakota Indian bands with a United States delegation headed by territorial governor Alexander Ramsey took place along the Minnesota River in 1851. Baker compared it to William Penn's purchase of the site of Philadelphia in 1683. The general felt that art had served history in that event, for it gained its fame in "the purely imaginary scene painted by Benjamin West." "Ramsey's treaty was as formal as a meeting of the Roman senate," Baker lectured the Board, "and was marked by all the negotiations of a solemn contract between independent nations. William Penn was most fortunate in his artist; we await the genius of our artist to perpetuate the scene of a greater treaty, on the walls of the most noble structure yet reared in the West."

Gilbert agreed with General Baker's suggestion, and first considered one of the lunettes in the stair halls as a suitable location. By the end of 1903, however, he was designing a place in the Governor's Reception Room for the treaty painting. He received other suggestions for themes from state history. Archbishop John Ireland recommended the discovery of St. Anthony Falls by Belgian friar Louis Hennepin in 1680. Civil War veterans wrote the architect, the Board, and the newspapers to press for paintings honoring the deeds of Minnesota regiments. With popular interest to reinforce his enthusiasm for interior decoration, Gilbert prepared more ornate plans. "I made new designs for the Governor's room to accommodate historic paintings in accordance with the sketches approved by the Board," he wrote to Seabury, and a St. Paul newspaper reported that "it is planned to make the Governor's room the most artistic."

Early in 1905 Gilbert sent Seabury a diagram for the placement of a whole series of Civil War paintings in the room. He advised the Board on subjects for the paintings, compiling a list of Civil War battles from his "inquiries among various officers who served in Civil War regiments." He recommended artists, and critiqued their work from first contract to final installation. When a self-appointed committee sought to commission a painting of the battle of Gettysburg, Gilbert fought them off in the name of artistic standards and maintaining the unity of his designs. He felt some urgency about making a full cycle of history paintings for the Reception Room: "It seems to me that if the Board does not cover the vacant spaces that somebody will get in their deadly political work later on and make that room a chamber of horrors in the name of patriotism." The history paintings that Gilbert clustered in the governor's suite vary in their individual impact and artistic success. But together, they comprise an effective primer of historical events that the Capitol's tour guides use each year in teaching thousands of Minnesota schoolchildren.

"I personally believe in historic paintings for such a room and I think they should be treated from the pictorial standpoint rather than the decorative standpoint," Gilbert wrote to Seabury, "they should really be pictures of the events as nearly as they can be transcribed." General Baker would find no "dancing nymphs or goddesses" here, but instead a series of scenes from the past built up from artists' research, interviews, and even reconstructions. Unlike the high-flown decorations adhered to the walls of other chambers, and conceived as two-dimensional adjuncts to their architectural settings, the Reception Room's history paintings are stretched canvases, physically and conceptually separate from the walls they occupy. The painters treated their assigned spaces in the Reception Room like windows that looked back in time, opening onto the battlefields and treaty grounds of Minnesota's past. Thus each scene has its own pictorial logic, its own perspective and lighting, without domination by its room setting. A decorator-muralist like Cox took pains to blend his work into its surrounding stone colors and light sources; a history painter like Francis D. Millet had the different task of staying true to the event he illustrated.

Millet's six by ten foot painting of the treaty signing at Traverse des Sioux hangs over the marble mantle at the Reception Room's west end. The artist was an accomplished painter of historical scenes, a journalist and war correspondent, and a successful muralist, who had supervised the work of many artists at Chicago's 1893 world's fair as its Director of Decorations. But like many American muralists, Millet later turned away from the allegories he lampooned as "customary representations, such as a group of young women in their nighties presenting a pianola." For his treaty painting Millet used the resources of published and eyewitness accounts, plus a painting of the event by an artist who had sketched the treaty in 1851. Frank Blackwell Mayer, a painter and librarian from Baltimore, recorded the treaty in drawings and diary entries:

> In an arbor formed of green boughs laid upon a frame work of young trees the commissioners of the U. S. & the chiefs of the Dacotahs met to treat. At one end on a raised platform was placed a table behind which sat the commissioners, the American flag hoisted behind them a few feet from the arbor, at the sides were the secretaries, reporters & to the right & left stood & sat on the ground the traders[,] half-breeds & spectators. In a semicircle in front of the commission, the chiefs were seated on benches.

After the treaty signing Mayer returned home, later painting murals for the Maryland statehouse in Annapolis. For years he urged Minnesotans to commission a mural of the treaty, even offering his sketch of it in 1885. Five years after Mayer's death in 1899, Gilbert (who recalled meeting Mayer in Baltimore) chose Millet to carry out Mayer's dream.

Millet went beyond a mere enlargement of the Mayer oil sketch. A stickler for detail, Millet sketched Indian headdresses and costumes, studied portrait photographs, and even built an arbor to Mayer's description outside his studio in England. But Millet depicted the treaty signing as a more sedate event than Mayer's words and pictures suggest. While eyewitnesses had noted frolicking children and howling dogs, Millet filled his canvas with attentive participants, including portraits of men who had become prominent in Minnesota public life. General Baker's wish for a painting to celebrate the treaty as Minnesota's key founding event was fulfilled.

Across the length of the Reception Room hangs another history lesson in paint: Douglas Volk's *Father Hennepin Discovering the Falls of St. Anthony*. The artist was something of a pioneer in Minnesota's art history. He founded the Minneapolis School of Fine Arts (later known as the Minneapolis College of Art and Design) in 1886. Volk painted portraits of Minnesotans before returning East six years later. Gilbert's recommendation was less informed by sentiment than by his awareness of Volk as "an artist of considerable reputation and very great ability." Volk's long-standing interest in painting scenes from colonial history was also important. "His work being more distinctly pictorial," as Gilbert wrote, it was well suited to the Hennepin theme. Volk created a solemn tableau to balance Millet's treaty painting. He read Hennepin's *New Discovery of a Vast Country in America* and N. H. Winchell's *Geology of Minnesota*. He examined a portrait said to be of Hennepin, in the collection of St. Paul railroad baron James J. Hill. He walked the banks of the Mississippi, where St. Anthony Falls had become the heart of a world-famous milling district. From these researches Volk composed a scene showing the priest raising his arms to christen the Falls in the name of his patron saint, while his traveling companions looked on. Volk credited Gilbert for details like the crucifix in Hennepin's hands, and asked his advice on other matters. "There is nothing more picturesque, perhaps, than fur, and I would enjoy painting a fur cap on Picard du Gay, as you suggest, but how about it in July?" wrote Volk in an effort to suit the costume of Hennepin's companion to the weather. The painting was the first to be hung in the Governor's Reception Room. "All beholders are immediately interested and charmed," noted *The Minnesotan*, a state art

Francis D. Millet's Fourth Minnesota Regiment Entering Vicksburg
hangs in the Governor's Reception Room.

magazine. "It is a mark of greatness in works of art that they appeal at
once to the common eye."

Popular appeal was a must for the remaining six paintings in the
governor's suite. Commissioned and installed between 1904 and
1912, the pictures pay tribute to what Garnsey called "Minnesota's
proud share in the battles of the Civil War." Gilbert surveyed the officers of Minnesota regiments to select subject matter, and recommended artists to the Board. As with the Capitol's allegorical murals,
his first choices (including Western artist Frederic Remington) were
not always available. But Gilbert's corps of painters—Millet, Volk,
Blashfield, Howard Pyle, Rufus F. Zogbaum and Stanley M. Arthurs—
brought experience and credentials to work that was done under
careful scrutiny. Senator William D. Washburn wrote an open letter
in a Minneapolis newspaper, proposing the battle of Gettsyburg as
one scene. Other officers were quick to remind citizens of the worthy
deeds of their own regiments. And enlisted men were among the crit-

ics, too, as Arthurs discovered on hanging his painting in the antechamber: "Soldiers who took part in the event are not pleased with
the painting in many respects. It is said that the blankets are not
properly arranged."

Gilbert chose for *The Battle of Gettysburg* an artist who made war
his specialty. Rufus Zogbaum, Gauthier noted, "has devoted twenty-
five years to studying and painting military and naval subjects, and he
has written many books on army and navy life." His subject was a
moment of tragic glory for the men of the First Minnesota Regiment,
who suffered tremendous casualties in halting a Confederate advance
at Gettysburg in 1862. A Minneapolis editorial seconded Senator
Washburn's call for a memorial painting: "No artist could ask for a
more inspiring theme. No incident in the history of the state is entitled to a more prominent place in the decorations of our new Capitol." Zogbaum, a seasoned war correspondent, gathered the stories
and portraits of Minnesota veterans and prepared dozens of detailed
drawings. He built his picture around the glare of an exploding shell,
past which dozens of soldiers charge.

Volk's painting of *The Second Minnesota Regiment at Missionary
Ridge,* a daring uphill fight in Tennessee, hangs opposite. This, too, is
based on battlefield visits and portraits. Volk used for his models not
just Minnesota veterans, but also the kind of war-torn flags that visitors can still see in the Rotunda. Minneapolis critic H. H. Kidder
noted how Volk matched sentiment with composition:

> In the general cold blue of the picture, the glowing warmth of red in
> the flag (like a symbol of hot blood and the patriotic daring that re-
> deems the cruelty of war) coincides with the placement, at the very
> centre of the design, of this symbol of Union as the whole cause at
> stake.

Howard Pyle's *The Battle of Nashville* is the acknowledged masterpiece of the Capitol's battle paintings. The popular author-illustra-
tor, known for his immersion in the spirit of his theme, said of a battle painting that "I felt the reality so vividly that I had occasionally to
go to the door of the studio and breathe fresh air to clear my lungs of
the powder and smoke." For his Capitol painting, Pyle consigned officers and flags to the rear of the muddy landscape. He focused instead
on the faces of the Minnesota men of four regiments who loom up to
the very edge of his canvas. *The Battle of Nashville* drove Gauthier to

a fit of alliteration in telling its "fierce action, impelled by a force of fanatical forgetfulness of self which makes heroes."

Not every Civil War painting is a tribute to "the patriotic daring that redeems the cruelty of war." Perhaps wary of assaulting viewers with unremitting battle, Gilbert also specified two scenes of Minnesota regiments on the march. Millet's second painting for the Reception Room shows *The Fourth Minnesota Regiment Entering Vicksburg*. Gauthier's guidebook listed the artist's military exploits, but found "it is an indication of his gentleness of character that he preferred to represent a peaceful phase of the Civil War." His painting also represents the price of battle, in its rendition of a blasted landscape and wounded civilians. One soldier in the line of march lifts his hat, in a gesture echoed by a black man, perhaps a freed slave welcoming the Minnesota troops.

The Governor's Private Office, adjacent to the Reception Room, is paneled in mahogany; its gilding is confined to the ceiling. Gilbert selected "cool greenish grey" paint for the walls above the wainscot, as a fitting background color for the gilded frames of early governor's portraits. As a formal space dedicated to the state's chief executive, the Governor's Office shows a combination of original colors and furnishings with personal touches. One recent governor hung a collection of porcelain plates on the walls, while another displayed his allegiance to the University of Minnesota with sports memorabilia around the room. Portraits of past governors have hung in the Capitol corridors since 1944, so Gilbert's green walls serve as backdrop to paintings of the sitting governor's choice. The office and its adjoining Governor's Business Office were restored and repainted in 1986, with original desks, sofas, and a revolving bookcase installed in the same locations one sees in a photograph from Gauthier's 1907 guidebook.

On leaving the governor's suite, the visitor can pause in the antechamber to view its two large framed paintings with a better feel for their place in the Civil War series. Stanley Arthurs painted *The Third Minnesota Regiment Entering Little Rock*. A student of Pyle and assistant on his larger commissions, Arthurs incorporated the requisite portrayals of Minnesota men into his view of the long column stretching across the Arkansas River. As in Millet's march into Vicksburg, an exchange of glances—here, between the Third's weary drummer boy and a straw-hatted young civilian—adds a tender touch.

The final battle scene to be hung in the governor's suite depicts a climactic moment of *The Battle of Corinth*, in which the Fifth Minnesota Regiment seizes a Confederate cannon. Edwin Blashfield, familiar to the Capitol visitor from his allegorical lunettes in the Senate chamber, here confined his art to real people in the heat of battle. The mural-sized canvas is signed by Blashfield and his assistants Vincent Aderente and Alonzo E. Foringer. Blashfield outlined this collaborative process in his book *Mural Painting in America:*

> It would be folly for him [the muralist] to consume his hours in going over vast stretches of canvas with paint. Once he has found his design, his shapes, his colors, his values, his assistants may put them upon the canvas for him, and when they have reached a certain point he too plunges into the thick of the fight and works with them, elbow to elbow.

Some viewers find it surprising that Blashfield's painting focuses the eye on a Confederate officer, standing unarmed against the Regiment's charge. As a reminder that bravery could be found on both sides of the conflict, the painting recalls the cautionary words of historian William Watts Folwell on the Capitol paintings: ". . . such memorials of a war between sister states in the American Union are not in good taste. The Roman custom of preserving no memorials of a civil war is one that America, now united forever, may properly follow."

Visitors find in the governor's suite the essence of 1905 reverence for Minnesota's past. Present-day necessities, like a modern telephone on the desk or a floodlight for videotaping press conferences, are discreetly placed about the rooms. One can imagine the Reception Room, in particular, as a space where Minnesotans were unanimous in preserving Gilbert's vision unchanged. But the room was the locus of public debate about Capitol preservation in the 1960s. During Governor Harold LeVander's term, Gilbert's red drapes and rotund leather furnishings were replaced with gold velvet curtains and armchairs of a modern design fitted with mustard-yellow upholstery. In 1968 LeVander, who had recently formed the Capitol area's planning commission, decided to close the Reception Room to the public. No permanent changes were planned, but the room would be converted to office use. Minnesotans objected to this stopgap solution to a space shortage. Historical Society director Russell W. Fridley, an effective leader in the growing historic preservation movement, warned that "If any room in the Capitol has established itself as worthy of preservation for the enjoyment of the public, it is this one." Working with legislators and civic leaders to dissuade LeVander, Fridley kept the Reception Room open to visitors. This decision helped pave the way for the reevaluation and restoration of many Capitol spaces in the 1970s. Historian Jo Blatti, reviewing the LeVander controversy two decades later, called it "the beginning of an historical perspective regarding the Capitol."

In the 1980s, the governor's suite was refurnished on the basis of historic photographs and other documents. The red drapes were reproduced, complete with their rich gold trim. Original furniture was found and returned to the rooms, and the walls of the antechamber and private office repainted in Gilbert's original "dull green with decorations in low toned gold." Visitors will find traces of ongoing restoration work as they conclude their tour with a look at some of the Capitol's unique, if less grandiose spaces. Many painted panels and stencil designs in the hallways show small rectangles of carefully scraped paint. These patches, revealing successive layers of paint down to the original colors and varnishes, result from a survey of the painted surfaces, done in all the Capitol's public spaces between 1985 and 1989. An expert in paint conservation correlated his microscopic analyses of the test patches to historic documents, to create an accurate guide for future repainting.

The walk downstairs to the ground floor takes the visitor below a playful motif of a trellis wound with grapevines, painted on the arched ceilings. At the foot of the stairs one finds a public hearing room that is a recent addition to the Capitol, built in a space below the Rotunda which was left unfinished in 1905. An early photograph of the room was labeled "the ghost chamber," probably for reasons Gauthier noted in her guidebook: "The crypt-like ground floor has a timbrel vault under the rotunda where the acoustic properties give a peculiar echo as one walks across the floor. The sound is as of someone closely following, and it can be heard only by the person walking." In later decades the space served as storage, offices, and as a hearing room. Its redesign in the 1980s retained Gilbert's star motif from the Rotunda floor above, and incorporated materials and colors meant to complement the Capitol's 1905 features.

The visitor finds original spaces adapted to later needs and attitudes throughout the ground floor and basement. Portraits of governors who have held office since 1951 hang in the ground floor halls.

The paintings continue tradition with a variety of representational styles. Edward V. Brewer's near-photographic realism marks the portraits of Governor C. Elmer Anderson and Governor Elmer L. Andersen. Society portraitist Frances Cranmer Greenman painted Governor Karl F. Rolvaag in thick, sketchy brushstrokes, a dashing style that leads some viewers to question whether the state paid for an unfinished portrait. Governors choose the artist to paint the official portraits, as well as settings that reflect a sitter's roots and roles. Governor LeVander stands with his inaugural address before the painting of Lincoln in the House chamber, in a portrait by Barbara Brewer Peet. Jerome Fortune Ryan's official portrait of Governor Rudolph G. Perpich shows an open pit mine in the background, for a forceful tribute to the governor's Iron Range heritage.

The cafeteria in the Capitol basement offers a taste of restoration history along with its meals. "The restaurant is rather unique," the *St. Paul Pioneer Press* reported in 1905. "Its decoration and style of architecture are fashioned after the rathskeller of Germany. It is decorated in light drab with fresco in green . . . the ceiling is deeply arched and at different intervals there have been painted Americanized German eagles." Gauthier's 1907 guidebook noted that "German quotations are inscribed over each arch," but a 1939 revision described the room in tones of pastel yellow, deep blue, and silver.

Events and attitudes of the intervening decades had led Minnesotans to paint over Garnsey's rathskeller theme. Anti-German sentiment during the First World War and the Prohibition movement of the same era both had strong support here. A state commission placed severe restrictions on expressions of German ethnicity, while the Eighteenth Amendment prohibiting alcoholic beverages was known as the Volstead Act for the Minnesota congressman who championed it. In this climate, slogans like "Esset und trinket, was ihr habt und denket, was ihr wollt" ("Eat and drink what you have, and think what you choose") were deemed inappropriate for the statehouse of a loyal and sober commonwealth. But traces of the Gothic-letter slogans, eagles, vines and squirrels were uncovered in the 1980s paint surveys. Still in use, the cafeteria awaits restoration in a more tolerant and preservation-conscious era.

Other basement spaces are the creation of work relief projects during the Great Depression of the 1930s. With the aid of funds from federal emergency programs, Minnesotans excavated low-ceilinged

American eagles and German inscriptions are painted on ceiling and walls of the restaurant in the Capitol basement, circa 1913.

areas around the Capitol's stone foundations to gain nine thousand square feet of usable space. Part of this found space became private dining rooms for the use of the governor and Supreme Court, each with its mural (by unidentified artists) of a rushing stream to bring a taste of the Minnesota woods into the dark basement rooms. The Court keeps its dining room under lock and key. The executive branch has turned its dining room over to the use of citizens, by appointment. The room was remodeled with plaid curtains, cheap paneling, and acoustic tiles in the 1960s. But its mural still offers a soothing backdrop for the meetings of a women's professional group, an Alcoholics Anonymous chapter, and other gatherings.

If the Rotunda is the heart of the Capitol, the basement halls reveal its nerves and sinews. Huge rough-hewn stone blocks form the walls; pipes, ducts, and cables run above the visitor's head to all levels of the Capitol and to its neighboring state buildings. A system of tunnels, also created through 1930s work relief projects, connects the Capitol to the State Office Building and the Judicial Center. State workers wishing to avoid subzero cold or summer heat use the tunnels for lunchtime strolls, as well as business trips on foot. But Capitol visitors will be wise to ascend, by stairs or elevator, to end their tour back on the first floor. Leaving by the main doors and the great granite staircase, visitors can feel the architectural ideals of a century behind them, and see before them the influence of the Capitol as a living part of Minnesota's civic life.

Touchstone for Minnesotans

$\mathcal{A}$ CAPITOL TOUR need not end at the front door. Many visitors take a heightened awareness with them, down the granite steps to the Capitol grounds. Primed by an hour's immersion in the art and history of the state, they find that expressions of shared values spill across the lawns of the Capitol area. Monuments in stone and bronze honor the past at all seasons, though the figures may be shrouded in snow half the year. If one happens to be at the Capitol on the day of a political demonstration or a holiday festival, gatherings of citizens in celebration or protest may be under way. The Capitol provides not just a backdrop for monuments and gatherings, but a benchmark against which citizens can measure their ideals and accomplishments. In literal terms, the statehouse serves as a touchstone of traditional design, time-honored materials, and fine craftsmanship. In symbolic terms, the Capitol is a standard of continuity: an embodiment of Minnesotans' commitments to democratic values, whether carved in stone or enacted in law.

Gilbert, the Capitol commissioners, and their fellow citizens were well aware of the potential that the Capitol grounds held. As the statehouse walls were rising citizens eyed the grounds as the perfect place for memorials. The Board's 1901 report noted:

> We have been frequently asked, by members of the Grand Army of the Republic [the Civil War veterans group] and others, whether we could not, in some way, respond to their testimonial, upon the new capitol grounds, to the memory of Minnesota's departed heroes . . . we have, in consultation with our architect, formulated a plan for a 'Memorial Approach' to the main front entrance . . . which, we believe, would fully respond to the requirement indicated, and at the same time, be a pleasing departure from the stereotyped monument or shaft.

Gilbert's city plans from 1903 to 1931 elaborated on this "memorial approach" as a key symbolic function of the Capitol grounds.

But in the years 1904 to 1906, Gilbert was concerned with completing his Capitol and embellishing its immediate grounds. Four great granite pedestals on the main stairway drew the attention of the press, as well as the architect. Animal sculptures might grace such pedestals, as they did on paper in Gilbert's competition drawings, and in reality at the great world's fairs at Chicago in 1893 and St. Louis in 1904. Gilbert wrote Seabury that he was discussing with several prominent artists "the possibility of making decorative sculpture in which distinctly American subjects should be used, such as the moose, the buffalo, the bull, the horse and the panther, etc." But he acknowledged the need for noble concepts as well as noble beasts: "we do not want to make it look like a museum of natural history, and the sculpture to be permanently interesting must suggest something more than the reproduction of an animal form, that is to say, there must be some underlying idea of which the figure is a true expression." The pedestals remain empty to this day, fulfilling the prophecy of a man who sought to sell Gilbert four bronze lions in 1906: "The tendency is to become accustomed to seeing the bare pedestals and grow cold as to the importance of ever having the intended sculpture." But monuments ranging from plaques to statues to sculptural environments have found their place on the Capitol grounds, in response to the people's wishes.

The first monument of a permanent and artistic character was a memorial to Governor John A. Johnson, placed in front of the Capitol steps in 1912. After the death of the popular governor in 1909, a memorial commission was empowered to seek donations for a Johnson monument, though no contribution could exceed one dollar. The people's affection for Johnson was made abundantly clear when the sum of nearly $25,000 was raised. With that fund in hand the commission selected Andrew O'Connor, an experienced hand in public commissions, for a larger-than-life statue standing on a pedestal that would feature figures of the workmen of four Minnesota industries. O'Connor's farmer, miner, iron worker, and timber cruiser were subject to the same scrutinies as the figures in the Capitol's interior artworks. Critics carped at the details of packstraps and the expression of the governor, but O'Connor's work eventually passed muster. Like the artistic program inside the statehouse, this first commissioned monument on the grounds was meant both to honor an individual and to celebrate the workers and resources of the state.

In 1928 a monument to Governor Knute Nelson joined the Johnson monument in front of the Capitol steps. The Nelson monument
matched its predecessor in height, materials, and the combination of
a standing bronze portrayal with other figures around the granite
base. Sculptor John K. Daniels used the figures to summarize Nelson's
life in bronze. The pedestal statues depict Nelson as a young Norwe-
gian boy just arriving in America with his mother, and as a soldier in
Civil War uniform. The story of one man's life is thus linked to a larger
message of immigrant opportunity and service. A third governor
stands in bronze on the Capitol lawn, thanks to the efforts of union
members whose contributions matched statehood centennial funds
to honor a populist hero. Amerigo Brioschi's eight foot tall bronze depicts Governor Floyd B. Olson on a simple granite base. Visitors will
recognize his striding, pointing pose from the official portrait in the
Capitol halls. The monument was dedicated on its site facing the
State Office Building on Labor Day, 1958.

Besides three governors of Minnesota, two discoverers of America
are honored in monuments in the Capitol complex. Both statues
stand as personifications of ethnic pride, in period costumes that
offer a livelier subject (for both artist and viewer) than the business
suits of the chief executives. A larger-than-life bronze of Christopher
Columbus by Carlo Brioschi stands on a granite pedestal that pictures his ships in low relief. The figure strikes a haughty pose in Renaissance dress, map in hand, across Cedar Street from the Judicial
Center. Commissioned by an association of Minnesota Italian-Ameri-
cans, the monument was dedicated on Columbus Day, 1931. Some
25,000 spectators, including students excused from St. Paul's public
schools for the occasion, attended its unveiling. A later generation of
the state's Italian-American citizens honored their forebears by raising funds to restore the Columbus monument in 1992.

A rival claimant to the mantle of "discoverer" stands in a park to
the west of the Capitol at University Avenue and Rice Street. Daniels'
statue of Leif Erikson also bears the title "Discoverer of America" on
its pedestal. The thirteen foot bronze figure, portraying the "Norse
explorer" in winged helmet, sword, and staff, was unveiled before a
crowd of 5,000 people during the Territorial Centennial of 1949.

The governors and would-be discoverers form an inner circle of
monuments around the Capitol building. The erection of the Veterans Service Building after World War II initiated another circle of

Dedication of the statue of Christopher Columbus, 1931.

memorials, which express their tributes in forms other than the easily lampooned bronze-on-a-rock genre of heroic portraiture. The
building was planned as a "living tribute," expressing the state's belief
that a center to assist veterans was a more worthy gesture than a
mere marker or statue. A Court of Honor radiating from the Veterans
Service Building provides simple granite piers for plaques that commemorate the sacrifices of Minnesotans in the armed forces. At the
center of the Court of Honor a rose garden refreshes the "living tribute" with flowers and fragrance each summer. Architect Brooks
Cavin also sought to grace the entrances to the veterans' center with
an allegorical marble figure and an unusual fountain sculpture. The
indefatigable Daniels carved *Earthbound*, a nine foot Michelange-
lesque "symbolic figure of man's struggle for freedom," for the south
side of the building in 1956. On the north side facing the Capitol, a re-

Alonzo Hauser's The Promise of Youth *in front of the Veterans Service Building, 1959. The Centennial Building is in the background.*

flecting pool holds a fountain in the form of a huge flower. The motor-driven petals can be opened to release a spray of water, and to reveal a female figure within the flower. Titled *The Promise of Youth*, the figure by Alonzo Hauser has often been scorned as irrelevant to veterans' concerns, and even obscene. Most visitors to the Capitol area will find the fountain dry and the petals of its sculpture partly closed, offering only a peek at the figure within.

Nearby, sculptures of the 1980s revisit the idea of a figural tribute. *Monument to the Living*, Rodger Brodin's twelve foot tall soldier of welded steel, wears the fatigue uniform of the Vietnam War era. The sculptor deliberately sited his figure on the ground, rather than elevating it on a pedestal. The 1982 sculpture stands with hands spread wide, palms up, in a melancholy pose that reinforces the question Brodin, himself a Vietnam vet, inscribed at the figure's feet: "Why do you forget us?" Across from the Transportation Building, one can meet *Charles A. Lindbergh, The Boy and the Man*. The 1985 sculpture by Paul T. Granlund portrays Minnesota's famous aviator in two figures: the barefoot boy who watched birds in flight along the Mississippi, and the "Lone Eagle" who was the first to fly across the Atlantic solo. Quotations from Lindbergh's later work as an advocate for conservation are inscribed on the pedestals. Set in a simply landscaped grove, the sculpture invites one to sit and ponder dreams and deeds.

Artworks of the 1990s sought to bring even larger environments for relaxation and reflection to the Capitol area. These works incorporate trees, pathways, lighting and benches to make the environments inviting and responsive to the seasons. Minnesota's Percent for Art Program, which helps artists and state agencies create artworks by the use of one percent of a building project's costs, played a key role in two ambitious projects. The Judicial Center, formed by new construction adjacent to the former Historical Society building, has a plaza designed by Richard Fleischner in 1991. Simple columns and shapes of stone accentuate a space that invites discussion along its paths and in an open-air meeting space. It also recalls, with minimalist cues, the setting of LaFarge's Socrates mural in the Supreme Court chamber. The largest memorial in the Capitol area is the work of a team of Minnesota artists. Through the Percent for Art Program, they created *Lake Front DMZ* as an entry to a memorial to the state's Vietnam casualties. Nina Ackerberg, Jake Castillo, Rich Laffin and Stanton Sears designed *Lake Front DMZ* to link Minnesota and Vietnam, artistically and emotionally. It leads the visitor past maps of Indochina and Minnesota to a memorial wall, inscribed with the names of the 1,120 Minnesotans killed or missing in the war. Dedicated in 1992 in a ceremony which featured a reading of the names of Minnesota's casualties, the memorial creates a world of its own within the larger Capitol complex. Visitors come alone or as families to remember loved ones, while larger groups convene on Memorial Day to pay their respects and leave offerings of flowers, notes, and mementoes.

In 1993, the Capitol Area Architectural and Planning Board adopted thematic groupings for artworks within the Capitol grounds. The CAAPB identified zones of the Capitol mall as especially well suited for "commemorative works." This strategy affirms Gilbert's

Minnesota's New Capitol, as pictured on a cigar box lid, circa 1905.

conception of a "memorial approach," and recognizes the logic of those monuments already built. The area closest to the statehouse is designated for memorials of governors, statesmen, and judges under this plan; military memorials would continue to cluster near the Veterans Service Building; and Minnesotans like Lindbergh the aviator would be honored along the John Ireland Boulevard axis. Plans for possible memorials to Hubert H. Humphrey and civil rights leader Roy Wilkins (who grew up near the Capitol in St. Paul's North End neighborhood) can thus fit neatly into the Capitol mall's landscape plans, while each can still have an aesthetic identity of its own.

The Capitol area has been Minnesota's essential gathering place for more than a century. St. Paul's first Ice Palace was built nearby in Central Park during the Winter Carnival of 1886. Festivals celebrating Minnesota's most salubrious season have occured periodically ever since. Another Ice Palace was built near the Capitol in 1937. Snow and ice sculptures in later carnivals have rivaled the size and scope, if not the permanence, of the area's bronzes. The ceremony for the laying of the cornerstone in 1898 was a prototype for gatherings to follow, as it combined political, memorial, and festive agendas into

*Snow sculpture on the Capitol Grounds during
the St. Paul Winter Carnival, circa 1985.*

one July afternoon. A parade opened the ceremony; blessings, speeches, and tributes filled the program; performances of Sousa's "Stars and Stripes Forever" and Rossini's "William Tell Overture" punctuated the proceedings.

In the decades since, the Capitol has offered an irresistible stage setting for demonstrations, protests, and rallies. The 1937 People's Lobby actions that culminated in the takeover of the Senate chamber began as a rally on the Capitol grounds. Farm protestors of the 1980s lined the streets of the Capitol complex with tractors to capture the attention of legislators and television cameras. Demonstrators on both sides of the abortion debate throng to the Capitol each January, to voice their opinions on the anniversary of the 1973 court decision that legalized abortion in America. Whatever the issue, such displays of citizens' convictions confirm the observation of *Minneapolis Star-Tribune* columnist Doug Grow: "There's nothing like the sense of power that comes from a rally at the Capitol."

Gatherings on the statehouse lawn transcend politics, too. Minnesotans celebrate here. Thousands joined in a ceremony of welcome and relief in 1981 when American hostages, including Minnesotan Bruce Laingen, were freed in Iran. A three hundred foot yellow ribbon, the national symbol of hope for the hostages, draped the Capitol façade as a grand gesture of support. When the Minnesota Twins won baseball's World Championship in 1987 and 1991, the Capitol was the destination of their victory parades. The Capitol area has also become the venue for events that regularly draw huge crowds. It is the finish line for the Twin Cities Marathon, a twenty-six mile race that brings thousands of runners and even more spectators to the Capitol each October. Benefit walks for causes like AIDS research raise funds and awareness, as they bring citizens out for mass shows of support. Memorial Day and Veterans Day bring time-honored ceremonies with speeches and music.

But the ultimate annual gathering occurs on Independence Day. Part picnic, part county fair, part theme park, and part Fourth of July celebration, the Taste of Minnesota festival has become the state's extravaganza of food, music, and fireworks. The festival began in 1983 as an attempt to draw people to the Capitol area, and succeeded wildly. As many as half a million people pour into the Capitol area for the four-day event. The fine points of classical architecture may go unappreciated while the streets are lined with fried-food booths and beer stands. But the image of the Capitol floats serenely in the background each night, as fireworks light up the sky. The morning after the festival, the Capitol area wears the look of a civic hangover of epic size. After the mountains of litter, kiddie rides, and portable toilets are removed and the streets steam-cleaned, Minnesota's front lawn is restored to its customary dignity.

The Capitol's calendar is ruled not only by the orbit of the sun, but by forces of custom and law. Visitors readily feel the influence of nature's seasons, but they can also sense the rhythms of the Capitol's human uses. Summer brings a blaze of color to flower beds on the grounds. Vacationers touring the state or the country stroll about the monuments, while kids from nearby neighborhoods occasionally use the Capitol steps for daredevil bike stunts. When winter snows bury the lawns, well-shoveled sidewalks still outline the broad geometries of the Capitol complex. In spring, the area seems to belong to schoolchildren. Lines of yellow schoolbuses ring the streets, and boisterous groups line up on the steps for class pictures. Autumn has a subtler atmosphere. Trees on the Capitol grounds change color as Minnesotans, known to sniff winter in the air as early as Labor Day, walk with brisker steps to their state buildings.

But the political calendar has its own season, when the state legislature is in session. "Session," as some call it in Capitol shorthand, is a season of intense energies. By law, the legislature operates in two-year cycles; the House and Senate may meet in both years of a biennium, for a total of 120 "legislative days" between early January and late May. But one may not need to check the date to know if the session is on. There are signs inside and out. Parking meters are hooded, to reserve spaces for elected officials and their staff. At the Capitol information desk, daily listings of committee meetings and hearings share counter space with tour brochures. A perceptive viewer can distinguish those who are at the Capitol to see and learn from those on more demanding business. In contrast to the tourists' casual dress and cameras, lobbyists in suits brandish cellular phones. The visitor who tours the statehouse while the legislature is in session witnesses politics in performance, on video monitors in the halls as well as from spectators' galleries in the Senate and House.

The Capitol remains a working building and a symbolic presence as it enters its tenth decade. Its story has not been one of unquestioned acceptance. As workers were moving into the new statehouse in 1905, some were deriding it as "a collection of misfit offices." "Already the building is jokingly spoken of as 'the beauty pile', and plans are being discussed for remodeling the interior," noted the *Minneapolis Journal* in an article entitled "Beautiful But Not Useful." But Minnesotans have shown their support for the building by patching its leaks, repairing its murals, and adapting its spaces to an ever-enlarging state government over the years. The Capitol has survived changing tastes, overcrowding, and even the zealous but sometimes imaginative interpretations of Cass Gilbert's original intent, a phrase that rings like a mantra through successive restoration plans.

Gilbert built a national career on the early fame he earned with his Minnesota State Capitol. He later designed hundreds of structures, some of which gained notable places in American building art. His Woolworth Building was an important Manhattan skyscraper, a modern structure cloaked in Gothic ornament. His United States Supreme Court building exemplifies the official classicism of Washington, D. C. Gilbert designed the art museum for St. Louis, the library for Detroit, and the capitol for West Virginia. He developed a master plan for the University of Minnesota's Minneapolis campus in 1910. An unrepentant traditionalist in the age of modernism, Gilbert was committed for life to his ideals of classical design, and to his Minnesota statehouse. Two small passages from his vast papers hold surprising messages with both humor and perspective, for those who care about the Minnesota statehouse and civic buildings like it.

In June 1904, Gilbert's aide forwarded a supplier's extravagant claims for a new style of lightbulb. The architect scrawled a reply: "I suppose this is one of the usual 'cure-alls' that will correct every defect and enhance every beauty, strengthen the masonry and improve the curvature of the dome—keep the roof from leaking and heat without fuel. . . ." Gilbert was well aware that there were no shortcuts, cure-alls or easy answers in building for the citizens of his day and of the future. He also knew that the Capitol and its makers would bear the brunt of artistic, economic, and political censures. He confided to Seabury, "We must not look for immediate praise in Minnesota, and we must not be disappointed if some criticism is made, but when they have time to consider I have no doubt that they will approve."

The building and its artworks have survived, despite such criticisms as art historian Donald R. Torbert's faint praise in 1958: "It was elaborate, expensive—and impractical, but it was much admired outside the state as well as within." Yet these very characteristics may have been the unlikely keys to the Capitol's acceptance through the whims of the fashion-driven, efficiency-oriented twentieth century. Minnesotans have taken their statehouse to heart, as a building that harkens back to a more self-assured era. *St. Paul Pioneer Press* architecture critic Larry Millett observed that in times past, "public buildings were seen as representing, to one degree or another, the broad ideals of society and the continuity of culture. The Minnesota State Capitol is a splendid example in this regard, offering a set of images intended to link the state and its citizens to the classical traditions of Western civilization." Yet Millett, writing in 1994, recognized that such a building was no longer likely to be built. The skills to build it are scarce or lost; the assumption of shared traditions is suspect among many citizens.

Minnesotans of the late twentieth century (like their fellow citizens nationwide) may indeed lack the monolithic confidence and monumental craftsmanship that built the Capitol. But they have neither demolished it nor copied it to meet ongoing needs for space and symbolism. They have instead taken pains to preserve their statehouse. They have oriented their new buildings to it: a main axis of the

History Center focuses one's view on the Capitol, and the plaza at the Judicial Center serves to strengthen its link to the statehouse. Minnesotans have extended the Capitol area, in design and planning, to a larger extent than even Gilbert may have finally dreamed possible.

In a century marked by frequent, often abrupt changes in architecture and public life, Minnesotans have established a tradition of commitment to their statehouse. Their Capitol, compared to the classical and Renaissance landmarks that inspired it, is a young building in a young commonwealth. But it has already served its citizens from the infancy of the automobile era to the crises of nuclear power. As a symbol of solidity amid the conflicts that are part of the democratic process, the Capitol will continue to accommodate citizens and attract visitors in the century to come.

For Further Reading:
A Brief List of Sources

*R*EADERS WISHING to learn more can examine a few titles about the Capitol, browse a wider selection about its state and national context, and delve into a huge amount of documentary material waiting to be used in future studies.

Three publications form the core of Capitol reading. Julie C. Gauthier's *The Minnesota Capitol: Official Guide and History* (St. Paul: Pioneer Press, printer, 1907) was revised numerous times into the 1930s. Her explications and illustrations make this an essential source of information about how the makers of the Capitol saw their work. The October, 1905 issue of *The Western Architect* also offers authoritative commentary. Devoted in full to the Capitol, this issue includes articles by Kenyon Cox and Elmer Garnsey. Neil B. Thompson's *Minnesota's State Capitol: The Art and Politics of a Public Building* (St. Paul: Minnesota Historical Society Press, 1974) is an excellent overview of the Capitol's birth amid political power games in Minnesota. Among many articles on Cass Gilbert's long career, Sharon Irish's "West Hails East: Cass Gilbert in Minnesota" (*Minnesota History*, Spring, 1993) is most relevant to the Capitol.

The reader can construct the Capitol's Minnesota context, past and present, from a selection of books on art, architecture and state history. *Minnesota in a Century of Change*, edited by Clifford E. Clark, Jr. (St. Paul: Minnesota Historical Society Press, 1989), is a collection of essays on many aspects of life in the state during the Capitol's decades as center of Minnesota civic life. David Gebhard and Tom Martinson's *Guide to the Architecture of Minnesota* (Minneapolis: University of Minnesota Press, 1977) will cue the reader to the Capitol's architectural context, from Cass Gilbert's other Minnesota buildings to the structures which have grown up around the statehouse. Larry Millett's *Lost Twin Cities* (St. Paul: Minnesota Historical Society Press, 1992) and Lucile M. Kane and Alan Ominsky's *Twin Cities: A Pictorial History of Saint Paul and Minneapolis* (St. Paul:

The Capitol at night with its original exterior lighting, circa *1912.*

Minnesota Historical Society Press, 1983) together give an excellent visual overview of the the Capitol's urban context.

   The broad artistic context of the Capitol's early years is well documented in the essays of *Minnesota 1900: Art and Life on the Upper Mississippi,* edited by Michael Conforti (Newark, Delaware: University of Delaware Press, 1994). The Capitol has a chapter of its own in Rena Neumann Coen's *Painting and Sculpture in Minnesota, 1820–1914* (Minneapolis: University of Minnesota Press, 1976). Its place within Minnesota's tradition of outdoor sculpture is documented in Moira F. Harris' *Monumental Minnesota: A Guide to Outdoor Sculpture* (St. Paul: Pogo Press, 1992).

   For an excellent sense of the Capitol's national context, see H.

Wayne Morgan, *New Muses: Art in American Culture, 1865–1920* (Norman, Oklahoma: University of Oklahoma Press, 1978) and Richard G. Wilson et al., *American Renaissance 1876–1917* (Brooklyn: Brooklyn Museum, 1979). A convenient survey of all the state capitols in the nation can be found in Willis J. Ehlert's *America's Heritage: Capitols of the United States* (Madison, Wisconsin: State House Publishing, 1993).

Unpublished studies and state reports offer a rich source of information and interpretation. The following theses offer insightful views of their respective Capitol subjects: William Towner Morgan's "The Politics of Business in the Career of an American Architect, Cass Gilbert, 1878–1905" (University of Minnesota, 1972); Scott Lyle Koch's "Cass Gilbert's Minnesota Capitol Approach Plan" (Illinois State University, 1975); Patricia Anne Murphy's "The Early Career of Cass Gilbert, 1878 to 1895" (University of Virginia, 1979); and Wade Alan Lawrence's "Herter Brothers and the Furniture of the Minnesota State Capitol, 1903–1905" (University of Delaware, 1987). "Attention to Detail: 1905 Furniture of the Minnesota State Capitol" (St. Paul: Minnesota Historical Society, Capitol Historic Sites, 1989) by Carolyn Kompelien, Kendra Dillard, and Sherri Gebert Fuller documents dozens of furniture specimens. Two state-funded reports prove that their genre can produce well-researched, lively documents: *The Minnesota State Capitol Complex, the 1940s to the 1980s* by Jo Blatti (St. Paul: Governor's Office, State of Minnesota, 1987), and *History of the Minnesota State Capitol Area* by Gary Phelps (St. Paul: Capitol Area Architectural and Planning Board, 1985/1993). *Minnesota State Capitol: A Preservation and Planning Study for Public and Ceremonial Areas* (St. Paul: Capitol Area Architectural and Planning Board, 1984) by Miller-Dunwiddie Associates, Inc. is a detailed study of the building's condition and restoration strategy.

The primary source materials relating to the Minnesota State Capitol are vast in scope and potential. Two major sources in the collections of the Minnesota Historical Society (MHS) are available for browsing or for sharply focused research, within sight of the Capitol itself. The papers of the Board of State Capitol Commissioners cover all facets of the building's genesis and construction, in items which range from detailed account books to Board Vice President Channing Seabury's acute and sometimes passionate letters. A full set of blueprints and construction specifications for the Capitol and its furnishings are also part of these papers. A parallel resource at MHS is the Cass Gilbert Papers, with the architect's correspondence about many aspects of the Capitol carefully organized for researchers. Gilbert papers at the Library of Congress and the New-York Historical Society also have important Capitol documentation. MHS has most Minnesota newspapers on microfilm, plus an invaluable listing of Capitol articles in Twin Cities dailies, Bonnie G. Wilson's "The Minnesota State Capitol, Planning, Design and Construction. A Bibliography of Materials" (1971).

Index

NOTE:
"CS" means color plate
"photo" means black and white illustration